FELLOWSHIP

Stories of Transformation through
Grace and Spiritual Friendship

B.J. Weber's 40 Years
in New York City

Edited by Sheila Weber

Soli Deo Gloria

Dear Milind—
   Thank you for sharing
your beautiful story in this book.
your and Ajung's friendship
means so much to us and we
hope you are encouraged by these
accounts of what the Lord has done.
   I John 1:3-7
Walk in the Light—
      with love—
Sheila and BJ Weber

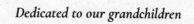

Dedicated to our grandchildren

Table of Contents

The New York Fellowship, 1985 to present

Introduction

By Sheila Weber

My husband B.J. Weber landed in New York City on a cold January day in 1979. He intended to stay for just a few months to test out working in a ministry to the poor and homeless. Surprisingly, 2019 marks his 40th year of ministry in the heart of New York City. A friend suggested that we recount just a few of the hundreds of stories and even miracles for the sake of posterity. So, I am taking the lead on this book in an effort to honor my husband. I hope to recount the ways that God is at work in all our lives through friendship and faith, and I pray our grandchildren will benefit from these stories as the years go by.

It is our hope that others will also be encouraged by what God has done throughout New York City from the time we both arrived in the late 1970s, when the city was dismal, churches were dead, and the place felt spiritually dark. We prayed for revival, and today we marvel at the abundance of flourishing new churches, new Christian leadership that has national reach, and evidence of souls awakening throughout NYC's five boroughs. (Best-selling author

Reverend Tim Keller of the now internationally-famous Redeemer Presbyterian Church held one of his first inquiry meetings in our living room. Hillsong now boasts up to 8,000 in weekly NYC attendance. The Christian Cultural Center in Queens has 35,000 members . . . and the list goes on.)

New York City is built on achievement, and the people who come here often have their professional goals first and foremost on their minds. But the stories that follow show lessons learned by others, that more important than their Ivy League credentials, more than their professional heights or political persuasions, and more than social reform or justice is the significance of relationships— relationships with one another and relationships with God. My husband B.J. and I each had our own years of youthful doubt, searching, and exploration—one of us in more extreme degrees and unconventional ways than the other. We came together in marriage partly because we had both discovered the same foundations of hope and meaning for our lives.

B.J. is almost 10 years older than I am; he was raised in the late 1940s and early 1950s small town culture of Dubuque, Iowa, where every family on his street had between four and eight children who manufactured their own fun—no summer camps for this crowd. Children flirted with danger on the Mississippi River, created their own baseball games, brought home fish and game to their family dinner tables, and had only one or two TV channels in black and white to watch the likes of "The Lone Ranger" and "The Ed

Sullivan Show." Remarkably, B.J. spent every Saturday morning quietly reading the "Book of the Week" club selection that his family ordered religiously . . . before he went out to collect night-crawlers for his fish bait business or gather his neighborhood posse on Huck Finn-like adventures.

B.J. had a larger-than-life reputation of being the town rowdy. He was not a bully, but he liked to stand up to bullies, meaning he was a really good street fighter. Because of B.J.'s antics and purportedly "disruptive" personality, he was often sent to the Dean of Students, Lefty Koob, who ended up becoming a good friend and mentor, encouraging B.J. through high school. There is more to tell, but suffice to say that B.J.'s classy, beautiful and wonderful mother, who loved him dearly, thought he needed to leave his hometown after high school graduation (and leave his father's aspirations that he get a union job at the meatpacking house), so that he could try to start fresh somewhere else. B.J.'s mother had grown up with privilege. She married the love of her life, her first husband, but tragically he was killed on the beach at Anzio during World War II. Her second marriage to B.J.'s father at times felt limiting and disappointing to her, but the marriage survived.

At 18, B.J. moved away and became one of the top salesmen at Anaheim Dodge in California. When the owner of the dealership told B.J. he could not date his daughter because she was only allowed to date college graduates, B.J. decided that he needed to be the first in his family to get a college degree. After saving a bundle of cash in California, B.J. returned to Iowa and entered community college, which led him into a four-year degree program at Iowa State. He eventually graduated, despite the upheaval of the anti-war movement, which temporarily interrupted his progress. During the national trauma of the Vietnam War, B.J. joined the underground movement, Students for Democratic Society (SDS), became a campus radical, and went to Canada for a season to flee the draft. Nearing the end of all the anti-war movement, he was ultimately classified 1Y, which he says meant you would only be drafted "when the Chinese cross the Mississippi River." But those days of cultural earthquakes also came with new trends of dangerous living, drugs, the birth control pill, uninhibited sex, and Woodstock (B.J. was there!).

Surprisingly, when I met B.J. so many years later, I had a complete understanding of the cultural storm he lived through, because when I was 11 years old, I had my own front row seat to the same events. During those years, I lived four blocks from the White House on the corner of G.W. University, where all the anti-war marches gathered. My father was a United Methodist minister and activist; we had 200 college kids staying in our church next door to our parsonage during all the anti-war protests and marches. We theorized that B.J. could likely have been standing on my corner, or marching right in front of my family's three-story townhouse since he attended all the D.C. protests and I lived at the epicenter of it all!

By 1973 B.J. had almost completed a PhD in child psychology with the explicit goal to shape (well, manipulate) the young minds and hearts of America toward the "beauty" of communism. He was teaching child development and running the preschool program at the University of Dubuque in his hometown. One day he drove out to a cloistered Trappist monastery, New Melleray Abbey, an enormous stone castle-like structure built in 1849, in order to buy some of their locally-famous homemade monk's bread.

That day, Father Mathias, the abbot of the monastery, saw B.J. with hair down to his shoulders, wearing a "Free Angela Davis" button, *Siddhartha* and Mao's *Little Red Book* in his back pocket (and a pocket full of weed, unbeknownst to the monk), and said "You look interesting. What are you all about?"

B.J. at first railed against the bearded monk, "Why do you care? You capitalist, colonialist pig." To which the gracious monk laughed and said, "Come on downstairs. Let's get a cup of coffee." A three-hour conversation ensued. After B.J. spewed his arrogant poison for a long while, and the monk patiently listened, B.J. finally asked the monk derisively: "Why are you here?"

"To love and serve Jesus Christ, my Lord and my God, and to pray for the world," Father Mathias replied.

B.J. said, "I get the Lord part—like Lord Krishna. But I don't buy that Jesus Christ is God."

"Oh yes he is, B.J., and only God in Christ could die on behalf of your sins. And you seem to be carrying a lot of burdens," the monk gently professed. He pulled a tiny New Testament out of his robe and read from Hebrews 11:1, "Faith is the assurance of things hoped for and the conviction of things not seen."

It was as if a lightbulb turned on in B.J.'s head. "I think I want that," said B.J. "But how do I get it?"

"You start with an act of contrition, meaning a contrite heart for the ways you have hurt others, even hurt yourself," said the monk. "And you invite Christ to come into your life and forgive your sins and start you on a new path."

As B.J. puts it: *I was on a journey. There were so many unanswered questions in my life. War and death only seemed to reflect the casualness of life, conversations merely drifted to the next party or next event. I felt an inner restlessness for answers, a desire for more. Herman Hess's book* Siddhartha *was juxtaposed to Mao's* Little Red Book. *But clever sayings don't change lives. I was interested in a paradigm shift. Something I could grasp, that I could hang on to.*

The way of the Buddha thrust me into deeper ambiguity. Established Christianity had very little appeal to me because it seemed based more on morality than spirituality. Everything was unsatisfying. Sex, drugs, even academics seemed pointless.

My encounter with an old monk in a remote monastery became a Holy Spirit moment in my life. God can flood us with His Presence and inexplicably He did that for me in that moment. Father Mathias reflected that invitation from the one true God. Father Mathias's presence and affection to a total stranger was deeply attractive to me, and opened my heart and my mind to God's work in my life.

So the old monk led B.J. through the Lord's Prayer, line by line, whose words B.J. had forgotten from his childhood days in the Lutheran church.

And B.J.'s life was changed forever on that wintery December 16th day of 1973.

B.J.'s own stories will fill another book about what happened in the days and years to come. He spent six years living as a non-vowed "monk" in that Trappist community, later helping the Trappistine nuns down the road with their farming, while those communities paid for B.J. to go to a Protestant-Catholic consortium of seminaries nearby in Dubuque, where he obtained his Master of Divinity degree.

In this collection, you will read from the dearest of men, now 82-year-old Father William Wilson, a former Trappist but now a long-married, Anglican bishop, who was a hermit monk at New Melleray and became B.J.'s mentor and theology teacher. In those early years, Father William was called out of his hermitage to serve as priest-in-residence for the Trappistine nuns nearby, and took his new student B.J. with him. You will read from some of the Trappistine sisters of Our Lady of the Mississippi Abbey, where the late abbess Mother Columba became B.J.'s spiritual director, leading him on matters of the heart, psychology, and lifestyle as his new-found faith developed.

After six years of living on both the monastery and abbey grounds, and attending the seven daily monastic offices and learning the contemplative order of St. Benedict, B.J. had never become a Roman Catholic, but in his heart he is comfortable within that community of faith. Mother Columba discerned that B.J. was destined to ministry but not as a celibate priest and not necessarily in the confines of the Catholic institution. After finishing seminary, B.J. was exploring where and how to work in ministry, but even a traditional protestant church setting did not seem the right fit for him. Mother Columba suggested he work with the poor. Her investigations led him first to reach out to Covenant House, a shelter for runaways in Times Square, New York City, but that group suggested that B.J. might have a more satisfying experience with the more overt Christian proclamation found at the nearby Times Square street mission called the Lamb's.

In this collection, you will read stories about B.J.'s first years in New York, where he moved in January 1979. We met a few months later in April, and married in August 1980. During our first five years of marriage we lived in the Lamb's, an old-fashioned Gospel

Mission for the homeless and destitute, which is why my own chapter in this collection is titled, "What were you thinking?" I got asked that question a lot in those days.

The Lamb's was an eight-story historic building designed by Stanford White at 130 East 44th Street, which for more than a century had been the famous Lamb's Club for actors. The likes of Fred Astaire had lived there, and Rodgers and Hammerstein wrote many musicals in that building. The Manhattan Church of the Nazarene purchased the building in the late 1970s, where it ran a ministry to the homeless, a food pantry, three floors of residency rooms rented to artists, actors, and musicians, and provided housing for its staff. The church held Sunday and Wednesday services in its gem of an off-Broadway theater—the altar, choir, and preaching were on stage—and our friend Carolyn Rossi Copeland built an outstanding award-winning theater program in that space, which ran successfully for decades. (Having been sold later by the church, the renovated property is now the luxurious Chatwal Hotel, where our once $50 a week single rooms now rent for up to $1300 per night.)

The late 1970s and early 80s were a dangerous time to live and wander the streets of Times Square. The colorful stories that follow will give you some of the flavor and drama of those street ministry days, but B.J. will have so much more to share in what we plan to be his forthcoming autobiography.

We stayed at The Lamb's for five years, and because neither one of us had a long-standing background or intended future with the Church of the Nazarene, in 1984 we moved 12 blocks away to an apartment in the Kips Bay/Murray Hill neighborhood of midtown Manhattan, and started a ministry called the New York Fellowship (NYF). The N.Y. Fellowship continues to this day and has been an outlet for B.J's creative style and his unusual capacity to serve both leaders and the needy alike.

We each have our own stories to share, but B.J.'s story is an unconventional and dramatic one. For now, we are privileged to let our friends tell some of the hundreds of stories, however truncated they must be. We hope you, the readers, find encouragement in knowing that change is possible, for ourselves and for others. We do not have to be stuck in our ways. God has a plan and a purpose for each of us.

Discovering that plan and purpose involves admitting that life is so much bigger than we think, honestly attempting to understand the life, teachings, atonement, and resurrection of Jesus, and reading the oft-forgotten but mind-blowing content in the world's best-selling book, the Bible. (If you are attempting this for the first time, start with the gospel of John . . . don't get bogged down in the Old Testament at first leap).

B.J. is living proof that self-discovery and restoration comes to full bloom when we make ourselves available to God.

We hope you are encouraged by the inspiring messages in this 40th anniversary commemorative collection. We are indebted and deeply grateful to all the many friends who have supported our life and work financially and prayerfully through the New York Fellowship all these many years, and for the years to come. And we give all the glory to God, whose faithful goodness and provision have surpassed anything we could have asked or accomplished on our own.

With profound gratitude,
Sheila Weber

SPIRITUAL ROOTS: THE MONASTERY YEARS

1973-1978

A Rebel Comes Home

By Emerson Eggerichs, Ph.D.

In my mind, I still see B.J. walking toward me inside a lounge area at Dubuque Seminary. It was 1975 and I was 24 years old. Someone had told him about me—that I was a guy who believed like he believed. Even then, I think he made a smart-aleck remark to me, something like "I bet you think you're some kind of big deal, huh?" I was taken aback at first because I didn't feel that way about myself. Then I saw the twinkle in his eye and realized B.J. was a jokester. I laughed and from then on, we were kindred spirits.

Our special bond was also confirmed by B.J.'s dog. He owned a Great Dane named Blue, and Blue knew we were kindred spirits. Why do I say that? I have the distinction of being uniquely favored by Blue. I love dogs as B.J. does, so once a week when I traveled to the seminary, I'd stay with Beej and "good ol' Blue dog." I jogged with Blue, played with him, and gave him treats under the table. At night, Blue slept next to me (I had the electric heater during the winter nights when the cold air drifted through the dilapidated farmhouse). On one occasion Beej raised his hand as though he intended to strike me as part of teasing Blue, and "good ol' Blue dog" aggressively growled and bared his teeth at Beej. I have never forgotten that snarl, nor has Beej. Beej was taken back that his own dog would "tease" back like that! At that moment, the authorization and adoption were official: I was family. Blue is now gone. Beej called me crying when he died. I cried too. Beej and I are family, and Blue knew that would always be the case.

During those seminary days, I learned of B.J.'s testimony. His story has stayed with me for decades. In a book I wrote, I shared the impact of his life on me and many others. You see, before hearing about Christ and opening his heart to the Resurrected Christ, B.J. Weber was a rebel. In the Bible, James and John, two later apostles, are called the "sons of thunder" before they yielded to the living Christ. The Beej would be of that genre. Here is what I wrote in my book, and what you need to know about how his story begins.

SUBMISSION FOR THE REBELS

God has great plans for some of you because he has made you a strong-willed person with incredible leadership abilities. The question is: Will you learn submission? If not, will you forfeit what God has in store for you?

B.J. Weber, the former chaplain of the Yankees, and my good friend since the 70s, talked to me about his days of rebellion in Dubuque, Iowa. As the town rowdy in his late teens and early 20s, he ignited trouble in most of the places he frequented. For example, one evening he set the record in the city for the most tickets—an embarrassing number of violations according to B.J. B.J. lived a reckless life to cover up his empty soul. He yearned for meaning, but could find no significance. Referring to himself as "a rebel in search of a cause," he joined SDS and actively participated in the anti-war and hippie movement of the 1960s. Nothing, however, could answer the deep questions in his heart.

Living in Dubuque, a heavily Catholic community with Trappistine nuns and Trappist monks, B.J. visited New Melleray Abbey to purchase homemade bread. While there, Father Mathias initiated a conversation with B.J. "You look like an interesting fellow. Tell me about yourself." B.J. wanted bread, not a conversation, so he said, "You aren't interested in me. Don't give me that!" However, the humble and loving Father Mathias didn't let it go. As the conversation continued, Father Mathias recognized that B.J.'s hunger for homemade bread paled in comparison to his hunger for the Bread of Life. As the dialogue deepened, the men discussed the purpose of life. Toward the end of their conversation, Father Mathias focused on the person of Jesus Christ and His claim to be the Son of the living God and Savior of the world.

Right then it was as though someone lit a match in B.J.'s dark soul. Frightened and exposed, he stayed in the light to feel its warmth and wooing. Could Jesus be the light of the world, he wondered? Could Jesus be the bread of life?

As he opened his heart to the resurrected Christ and asked Christ to save him from his sins, something good happened. A holy cleansing came over B.J. His shame and defilement from evil behavior lifted. B.J. became a Christ-follower.

Sometime later, B.J. eventually moved onto the farm to serve the monks and nuns. Mother Columba, head of the convent, took special interest in this new believer who had entered Dubuque Seminary, which is where I met B.J. in 1975. Like a mother, she regularly counseled him in the things of Christ. So, when Sherwood Wert of Billy Graham's Decision Magazine heard B.J.'s testimony and invited him to share it at a Billy Graham crusade in Cincinnati, Ohio, B.J. hurried to the convent to inform Mother Columba of this incredible invitation to share Christ with thousands. "What do you think, Mother?"

"B.J., this would ruin you," she replied. "You're too young in the faith. You should not do this."

Shocked, B.J. naively replied, "Well, I'm going to do this."

"If you do," Mother softly relayed, "know that we will always love you, and you can visit us, but you must leave our community."

B.J. was stunned. He could not believe what his ears were hearing. Frustration and hurt pulsed through his body. After a few moments, he retorted, "Well, what do you expect me to do?"

"I expect you to immediately go to the sheep barn and clean out all the stalls."

At that moment, B.J. the Rebel had to make a decision. Would he submit to her spiritual wisdom and authority, or pursue what he considered the opportunity of a lifetime?

With his head down and his shoulders sloped, he got up and walked to the sheep barn. For the next six hours, he did nothing but clean. However, God was also cleaning. While B.J. worked on the stalls, God worked on B.J.'s soul. B.J. recounts:

> Strangely, after a couple hours of battling, an unexplained joy descended on my soul. I knew that I needed to learn to submit. I knew I needed to follow the counsel. In that sheep's barn, the Shepherd met me. He sheared the wool from my eyes, and I am eternally grateful. I look back over three decades and sing his praises for my decision to submit. My heart mattered to my Lord far and above my ministry for my Lord. If I had not learned to submit, as you say 'respectfully doing what was rightfully required of me' when I did not want to do it, I do not believe my ministry in New York on the streets with the poor and the prostitutes, and then onto Wall Street with the prosperous and the professionals, would have lasted.
>
> I chose to submit to Jesus in the face of temptations and trials, having learned submission by scrubbing sheep's manure off a smelly stall floor. That moment of submission opened unique doors

far greater than Billy Graham's Cincinnati Crusade, as significant as that event proved to be for others.

Rebels need to hear B.J.'s testimony, especially those who are ambitious, highly concerned about status, and disgruntled by delays. While eventually many of these rebels rise to leadership positions, God often tames them through the discipline of submission so that they do not mess up future opportunities. Scripture warns that when you make wrong choices early on, refusing to submit to God's ways, then "you groan at your final end" (Proverbs 5:11).

This is the B.J. Weber I have come to love and respect. You will too as you turn the pages in this tribute to 40 years of ministry. I'd say Beej is a pretty big deal. I think you'll find him a kindred spirit.

Emerson Eggerichs, PhD is author of the *New York Times* bestseller *Love & Respect*, which was a Platinum and Book of the Year award winner and has sold more than 2 million copies, now expanded with other *Love & Respect* series, books, workbooks, DVDs, and podcasts. He and his wife Sarah are nationally renowned speakers.

The Trappist Hermit Monk

By Father William Wilson

God has used B.J. to shape my life in the Spirit and in the world. He never tried to do so. To tell you how this happened I must give you a vignette of my life.

Growing up as a child in Philadelphia, I developed a powerful impression that my family was messed up, including myself. That is not surprising. I was never quite sure who my biological father was. The man whose name I inherited, Bill Wilson, never denied that he was my father. But since he always ran around with women and became a homeless alcoholic on the street, Mom—who was a controlled alcoholic—tried to find some male companionship with other men. Dad had no religion. Mom was a fallen-away Roman Catholic.

When puberty asserted itself in my life, I could not understand it, much less control it. Meanwhile, I unfortunately mis-learned about sexuality in the alleys and vacant houses in our poor inner-city neighborhood. What I was taught on the street was a total degradation of sexuality as intended by the Creator. My education about sex at the local Catholic school I attended through 12th grade was quite different. In those days, we were told it was a mortal sin deserving of eternal damnation in hell even to entertain one explicitly sexual thought. I prayed and tried with all my might but I could not completely abstain from exploration of my emerging sexual impulses. That weakness made me feel I was sinful, dirty, guilty, and "worse than an animal" as one priest called me.

As far back as I can remember, God was always real to me. I thought about God. I talked to God. I wanted closeness to God. But I misunderstood my normal emergence into puberty as entrance into moral turpitude. I became filled with guilt and self-condemnation. For about a year, I thought about how I might put an end to my unceasing mental anguish by taking my own life. I planned several ways to kill myself. The shiny subway rails had a morbid attraction as a possible way out. I remember standing at the edge of a pier on the Delaware River. It was a dark rainy night. I looked down at the foul-smelling water, mulling over Hamlet's question about whether "to be or not to be."

In that very season, God brought a sweet girl into my life, and He surrounded me with two new great friends. Those relationships got me past my desire for death.

A year or so later, at nineteen, God orchestrated a convergence of circumstances that brought me into a Trappist monastery as a novice. Here, I could seek consummate union with God in silence, solitude, and separation from the world. The practice of perfect continence was an absolute requirement. If I failed, I would have to leave the monastic life. I prayed very hard for the gift of perfect continence. I repressed as much consciousness of the sexual dimension of life as possible. Whether by the force of repression or the influence of supernatural grace, I enjoyed perfect total abstinence from sexual actions and fantasy for seventeen years. The successful practice of the vow of celibacy in thought, word, and deed produced in me the feeling of purity and innocence that I so desperately lacked. After being judged "worse than an animal," I was now, all of a sudden, "pure as an angel." From the first day of successful continence and continuing for those seventeen years, I thought I was sexually perfect by controlling myself completely. But I was to find out that no one comes to sexual moral maturity simply by abstention.

In that fateful seventeenth year of my monastic profession, having completed all my studies in philosophy and theology, and having pursued the life of contemplative prayer with all my powers, while living as a solitary monk in a cabin in the monastery woods, my sexual perfection suddenly collapsed.

In my eleventh year as a monk, I was permitted to establish myself as a hermit monk on monastery property a few miles distant. I lived in a ten-foot by twelve-foot cabin, drank water from a stream, and lived on dried foods and canned goods. My unique ambition was this: to find through personal experience how deep and how constant a man could be conscious of God in prayer, scripture, and meditation. For several hours a day, I practiced what is known as hesychastic prayer—consisting in a simple silent invocation of the Lord Jesus in the heart.

Once, on my monthly overnight visit to the monastery, I was called upon to hear a confession. A Catholic priest never denies such a request. The penitent turned out to be a woman. I will be brief: I fell infatuatedly in love with her. She came every month when I was to be at the monastery. In my inner man, I wanted to love her 'pure and chaste from afar.' But I found myself unwilling or unable to resist when she drew physically close to me. There occurred some fleeting inappropriate touching—for which I was thrust back into feeling the guilt I had left behind so many years earlier.

I was sent to a monastery in Missouri to help care for an invalid monk who was dying. On my return, circumstances converged that I had to change buses in the city where she lived. She met me at the bus station and offered to get me something to eat during the five-hour wait until my bus connection back to the monastery. At her home alone together, our physical contact went beyond mere "inappropriate touches," and I knew it was sin.

On the four-hour bus ride back to the monastery, the gravity and the irreversibility of my sin descended like a cloud in my soul. I was a fallen monk, a priest unfaithful to his promise of celibacy.

I had broken my vows. I had betrayed Jesus. I had failed the covenant of monastic brotherhood that I owed to my community of monks. There was no repair. I felt spiritually lost. What happened to all those days and years of seeking His face in prayer? What about all the innumerable conversations of love I had had over the years with our Lord Jesus? What is left of my relationship with Him?

My first positive thought was to confess my sin to the Abbot as soon he arrived at the monastery. I would confess and accept whatever penance he would give me. I would even leave the monastery if that was his decision.

When I arrived at the monastery it was already late and the monks had begun the great silence when no one speaks. I learned that I could not go to see the Abbot because he was traveling out of state on matters of the Order. So, I loaded up my duffel bag with supplies and set out to walk the three miles to my hermitage. However, as I left, a young man with long hair and a very large dog greeted me. It was B.J. He was going home after visiting another monk, Father Jim. He offered to drive me to the end of the gravel road, halfway to my hermitage.

Sitting in the passenger seat, I felt a strong urge to confess my sin to this new Christian. In a way, I was unconsciously using him to alleviate my guilt. It was a pastoral indiscretion for me to unload on this young man new to the faith. I told B.J. what had happened earlier that day. He expressed feeling sorry for me, but otherwise was not shocked with scandal. At parting, I remember asking him to join me in the Lord's Prayer—which he had not yet learned by heart.

I arrived at my hermitage just before nightfall. I felt like a stranger in the little building that had been my home for years. I was not the same person who left it just a few days before. I did not know who I was now. I had enjoyed a comfortable relationship with God in my many hours of daily contemplative prayer. But now, having failed God so miserably, I did not know how to address Him. I just prostrated on the floor and cried. At some level, I knew in faith that God forgave me on account of the crucifixion of Jesus. But I could not forgive myself.

My whole world had changed. I felt like I had to do something different. I couldn't go on pretending to be a good solitary monk dedicated to God. I lost my identity as a man of innocence and virtue. I had become a grievous mortal sinner. I thought it might be an honest thing to do if I just walked off into the distance and became a homeless nameless wanderer.

I could not sleep very much. On the second day there, while I was lying prostrate on the floor, trying to speak to God but not knowing what to say, I was startled by the loud sound of what turned out to be B.J.'s Great Dane jumping onto the board outside my door. I immediately guessed B.J. would be right behind. "Oh

God," I thought to myself, "that young man I spoke to about my sin is coming out to give me counsel that I do not want! What a mistake I made in telling him!"

I opened when he knocked on the door. My intention was to be as brief as possible with him. In an annoyed voice I asked, "What do you want, B.J.?" He stood there; his facial expression was tentative, almost embarrassed. He replied: "I have decided to become a Christian and I came out to ask if you would be my teacher." As soon as I heard this, I was convicted of my own self-preoccupation. For the first time since my sin, I gave my attention to someone other than me. Without thinking, I just said, "Yes." If I had thought about it, I would have told him "No," because I felt unworthy and unfit to teach anybody anything about Jesus and His Father.

B.J. came out to the hermitage almost every day—with his big dog, Blue. I forgot about myself and my sin. I just poured myself into the young man who was hungry—even passionate—for God. Becoming B.J.'s first teacher did not resolve my grave personal problem of identity. It just changed the subject completely. I grew to love B.J. and I knew he loved me, although we never said anything like that. Monks were not supposed to love any person individually. Monastic fraternal love was thought to be a general attitude toward all people equally. "Particular friendships" were forbidden in the monastery. Without conscious intention, B.J. taught me the supreme spiritual value of friendship love, which the monastic culture had lost. The re-discovery of friendship enabled me, many years later, to love a wife and children and people in the world in total harmony with loving God. Later in life, B.J., unwittingly and unintentionally, introduced me to a doctor interested in medical mission who became my wife. The same B.J. called us and asked us if we were interested in adopting an unborn child who became our son, Will.

Based on my work in Bolivia, B.J. started the Amistad Mission in the United States. Thirty years later, the mission continues to save abandoned babies and children.

Do you wonder what happened to my relationship with God that was broken by sin? Well, at the end of my life God brought me to the place where B.J. began. Stripped of a relationship with God based on good moral behavior, I have come to accept myself as a sinner. Like all other sinners, I live in union with God by the grace of Jesus Christ. My relationship with God is established by the Precious Blood shed for sinners like B.J. and me.

Father William Wilson lived 25 years in the monastery before he moved in 1982 and lived as a Trappist among the poor of Bolivia. There he founded what would later become The Amistad Mission, building a clinic and school in the Andes Mountains, an orphanage in Cochabamba, a retreat house, and so much more. In 1989, he married Dr. Susan Winchester, who had been seeking to serve in medical missions with the poor. They now reside in Birmingham Alabama, have raised two children, and have been happily married for 30 years. Father William is still in active ministry through the Southern Fellowship, and is a retired bishop in the Anglican Church of South America.

My Rugby Nemesis

By George Getschow

I remember when I first laid eyes on him, across from a wind-swept Iowa schoolyard turned into a rugby pitch. Even at 50 yards away, I could see his sprawling shoulders trying to escape his skin-tight rugby shirt emblazoned with DUBUQUE RUGBY CLUB on the back. Above his shoulders, another freakish feature stood out from all the players circled around him—his neck. It protruded from his shoulders like a small tree trunk, and it propped up a humongous head that looked like it might have been stolen from Hercules. Yet, oddly, I remember I wasn't terribly fazed by this muscle-bound he-man until I heard his husky voice roar across the rugby pitch like it had been shot out of a canon.

"Let's kill 'em, boys!"

B.J.'s war whoop set in motion a bloody hour and a half-long battle that left my team—the Mason City Rugby Club—more pulverized than the coal dust billowing from Mason City's power plant. B.J. and his rugby ruffians saw to it that the star center back of Mason City's team (me) wouldn't gain an inch of turf. In fact, I'm sure I still hold the team's record for the most yardage lost in a single game. My mauling on the rugby pitch was my first direct encounter with B.J. Weber. Of course, I had heard of him. Everyone who attended Iowa State University in the early 1970s had heard of him. B.J. was a renowned street brawler, drug peddler, Vietnam War protestor, and provocateur.

Even when his rugby rowdies won, he was the consummate badass. At a bawdy rugby party following my team's drubbing, B.J. wanted to rub our faces even deeper in the dirt. He challenged my team to an arm-wrestling match to determine who would pay for the second keg of beer. We lost. After the party, Mason City's coach, a samurai warrior and swordsman who appreciated B.J.'s bravado and barbarity on and off the rugby pitch, asked me what I thought of B.J. I spit on the ground. "Well, Otomo, let's put it this way: If B.J. and I were the last survivors on planet Earth, I would live on the farthest side of the planet from where he lived."

* * *

A year and a half later, in 1974, I left Mason City to take a staff reporter's position in the Chicago bureau of *The Wall Street Journal*. I had barely settled into my new job when I picked up the phone one morning and nearly fell off my chair. It was the lusty voice of my old nemesis. "George, this is B.J. I've been thinking about you."

I couldn't catch my breath. I started panting. I felt like I might faint. There might have been a half-dozen reporters at their desks, and I could see their eyes fixated on me, like they were watching someone's skin fall off. "I'm really busy at the moment B.J.," I babbled. "I'll call you back as soon as I can."

I rushed to the men's room, trying to gain my composure. *What does that lout want from me,* I wondered.

Whatever it was, I knew it wasn't good. A small stake in a big drug deal he was arranging with Chicago's Gambino mob family in return for an unlimited stay in my guest bedroom? A shiny Cadillac off his father's used car lot in exchange for a $15,000 loan? My mind conjured up all kinds of dreadful plots masterminded by Dubuque's legendary hooligan— all at my expense.

I asked *The Wall Street Journal's* switch board operator to screen my calls. "If someone who goes by the name B.J. calls me, tell him you're happy to take a message, but that I'm unavailable— indefinitely." That afternoon, and every day for the next two weeks, B.J. called and left a message with the switchboard operator asking me to return his call. I never did. But B.J. managed to slip through my line of defense one day by calling himself a "Dr. Weber" who had a very urgent and confidential message for "Mr. Getschow" that he had to deliver directly.

"George, don't hang up," B.J. implored. "I've got something important to talk to you about."

God only knows why I didn't hang up.

"What is it, B.J.?"

"I want you to come up to Dubuque this weekend to meet two special people—a hermit monk and a cloistered nun who are my mentors and spiritual directors. I promise you they will give you the kind of guidance and direction on how to live a meaningful life that you won't get anywhere else on earth."

"Let me think about it, B.J.," I said, "and I'll get back to you."

B.J.'s voice stiffened. "No George. My invitation isn't something to think about. It's something you have to act upon now. You won't regret it."

B.J.'s invitation to meet his Catholic mentors and spiritual directors didn't make sense. He wasn't even Catholic. I kept asking myself, *Why was B.J., one of Iowa's preeminent hustlers, hanging out with a Catholic monk and a cloistered nun and why were they willing to put up with his deeply-rooted carnal instincts?*

Curiosity—my fatal flaw—got the best of me. "Okay," I said. "I'll see you Saturday."

* * *

B.J. stood outside the heavy wooden doors of the tiny Trappistine Abbey perched on a bluff overlooking the Mississippi River. Inside, I could hear the mellifluous voices of the nuns singing a Gregorian chant in perfect harmony. "Welcome to my new home," B.J. said, opening one of the doors and escorting me across a foyer filled with religious statuary and crucifixes. B.J. knocked on a door tucked behind a giant statue of the Blessed Virgin. There was a metal engraving with the name "Abbess" on the door.

"Mother Columba. It's me, B.J. May we come in?"

"Hi B.J.," said the nun, walking out from behind her desk to give him a hug.

"And you must be George," she said, smiling as she shook my hand. "B.J.'s told me all about you."

I wanted to say, *But B.J. hardly knows me, Sister, and I wouldn't trust anything that savage told you anyway.*

I kept those thoughts to myself.

Pleasantries aside, Sister Columba wasted no time giving her tell-all account of B.J. "A lost soul," she called him, who might well have ended up at the bottom of the Mississippi River entombed in a barrel of cement if he had not made a trip to New Melleray Abbey to buy a loaf of the monks' heavenly, hand-made bread. On this trip, B.J. wasn't looking for salvation. In one back pocket he carried a copy of the *Little Red Book* by Mao Tse-tung, the barbarous chairman of the Chinese Communist Party, and a stash of drugs in the other pocket. A portly, bearded monk named Father Mathias approached B.J. and offered him a cup of coffee. The three-hour conversation that followed inside the cavernous Gothic monastery would unravel B.J.'s unwavering fidelity to communism and his clenched-fist animus for Christianity.

In her long black habit, a hand-carved crucifix hanging by a strap over her shoulders and a perpetual smile as radiant as the morning sunrise, Sister Columba came across as the kind of lady who, stepping outside into the lovely landscape around the convent, might attract hummingbirds looking for a warm and tender place to nest. Even as a hard-nosed, cynical reporter covering all kinds of skullduggery and scandals for *The Wall Street Journal*, I was struck by Sister Columba's telling of B.J.'s "conversion experience" as being sincere, even inspiring.

Still, after leaving her office, I couldn't shake my doubts about B.J. Was Sister Columba being duped by the charming charlatan now claiming that his love of Jesus had conquered his decadence? How would she know if B.J. wasn't another Rasputin, the sexually promiscuous and immoral Russian peasant who styled himself as a holy man?

* * *

B.J. said he had some farm chores to tend to for a few hours—bailing hay and pulling weeds from the sisters' organic vegetable garden—but would return around 6 p.m. for our visit with the hermit monk. Meanwhile, he suggested I walk the "sacred grounds" of the Abbey, visit the chapel, and pray for a spiritual awakening and peaceful spirit during my time in Dubuque.

The soothing, honeyed tone of B.J.'s voice threw my mind into a tizzy. This was the same sadist who stirred up his team of ruffians to "KILL!" me and every player on my rugby team. Now he was hoping I'd obtain a "peaceful spirit" and some sort of personal transformation during my time at the monastery. While waiting for B.J.'s return, I walked the rolling farm fields and woodlands surrounding the nunnery. I spotted quail and pheasants, grouse and doves, coots and red-tailed hawks, even a few turkeys. I meandered across a meadow filled with wildflowers and honeybees. And I visited the nuns' candy shop, which produced the most exquisite caramels on earth. I bought two boxes, one to take home. But my sweet tooth got the best of me. Both boxes were emptied in the time it took me to walk around a tranquil pond covered with lily pads and frogs.

But neither my walk around the "sacred grounds" or gouging on the nuns' caramels brought renewal or a peaceful spirit. Instead, while waiting for B.J., I grew anxious, even agitated. I started asking myself, *Why are you here? What's the point of this? I could be hanging out with my friends at my favorite pub in Chicago, drinking beer, chasing girls.*

When B.J. finally arrived, after the appointed hour, I told him I had enjoyed meeting Sister Columba and walking the grounds of the convent. But I was tired and eager to return home. B.J. put his foot down. "George, you can't leave. Father William is expecting us. I promise. Our visit won't last long."

B.J.'s somber gaze melted my resistance. "Okay," I said. "As long as it won't be long."

* * *

B.J. used the nuns' communal automobile to drive 20 miles across gravel roads to the public parking lot of New Melleray Abbey. From there, we had to hike about a half mile up a steep hill and through a thick grove of bur oak and silver maple to reach our destination: Father William's hermitage.

The hermitage didn't amount to much. It was a 12-by-12 foot wooden box sitting on rough beams and planks, shrouded by a thicket of trees and brush that would make it hard for even chipmunks to find it. The inside of the hermitage consisted of a miniature wooden table and chair, a shelf mounted on one wall containing a Bible, a book about the ancient Desert Fathers, a canister of instant coffee, and a jar of peanut butter. There was no refrigerator or stove. I figured the monk must survive on cold coffee, peanut butter, and maybe honey from a local hive.

I suppose I shouldn't have been surprised by the hermit's Spartan living quarters. The monk was following the customs and religious practices of a group of early Christian ascetics who lived in the desert of Egypt during the 3rd century. The Desert Fathers became the model of Christian monasticism. With his unruly beard and rumpled tunic, the short, sturdy, and soft-spoken hermit looked in many ways like a modern-day Desert Father. Like the early Desert Fathers, the monk had committed his life to asceticism, silence, and unceasing prayer all day, every day.

As I would soon discover, he had also committed to converting me from a life centered on the pursuit of making money and merriment to making Jesus the focal point of my life. For the next eight hours, cornered by B.J. on one side and the hermit monk on the other, I received a crash course in living a meaningful, Christian life. The hermit's incantations on creation and death, mystery and mysticism, renunciation and self-realization, suffering and sacrifice, sucked the oxygen out of the hermitage with what felt like 10 tons of burning incense. I feared I might suffocate if Father William's sermonizing went on much longer. I had no doubt the hermit was talking about important stuff—the sort of grave and ponderous matters of the soul that, if taken to heart, would make the world a much better place. That's why I tried so hard, at least for the first few hours, to absorb the monk's mind-boggling erudition on the complex contents and tenets of the Catholic faith. But as the night wore on, my mind turned into mush and most of the monk's dazzling spiritual insights disappeared like constellations of stars in the early morning light.

The climax of my dramatic encounter with the hermit came around 3 a.m. "Do you want to accept Jesus as your Lord and Savior, George?"

"Yes!" I proclaimed.

I wasn't lying, exactly. I did want to. Just not then . . . another time . . . please God . . . when I'm not so dog-tired.

The hermit cupped my hands and blessed me with words that have stayed with me for the last half-century.

"George, Jesus loves you, more than you know, no matter how many times you fail him. He always has and he always will."

As I followed in B.J.'s footsteps on our walk back to the monastery through the woods, I remember thinking that he and his hermit had failed in their mission to convince me to make Jesus center stage in my life. I left Dubuque at the crack of dawn and headed home to Chicago, anxious to resume my life of work, rugby, and women.

But during the days, weeks, months, and years that followed, I never forgot that night in the woods. Something did happen there—something mysterious, something mystical. The hermit and B.J. had planted a seed in my head that continued to grow— the notion that God loves me, despite my flaws, despite my failings, even despite my inability to love Him as much as I knew I should. That belief is the pillar of my spiritual life today. B.J., now the charismatic leader of an influential group of Christian businessmen in New York City, and the hermit, now an Anglican Bishop in Birmingham, have become two of my best friends. Our friendship endures and grows stronger each year even though our paths seldom cross. What binds us is our common belief that we're all heading toward the same destination "in Christ Jesus."

George Getschow is the co-founder and director emeritus of the nationally acclaimed Mayborn Literary Nonfiction Conference, and co-founder and former editor of *The Best American Newspaper Narratives* and *Ten Spurs,* an award-winning literary journal. In 2012, Getschow was inducted into the Texas Institute of Letters for "distinctive literary achievement." He spent 16 years at *The Wall Street Journal* as a reporter, editor, bureau chief, and as the paper's Mexico correspondent. He also worked on the paper's Page One Rewrite Desk. Getschow is a Pulitzer Prize finalist and winner of the Robert F. Kennedy Award for distinguished writing about the underprivileged. George served as a Pulitzer Prize jurist for feature writing in 2013 and 2014 and for General Nonfiction in 2017. He is completing a book, *Walled Kingdom*, for John Macrae Books, an imprint of Henry Holt and Co., which grew out of two narratives he wrote for *The Wall Street Journal.*

The Monastery—
First Steps of Growth

By Sister Lillian

Our monastery in Iowa, Our Lady of the Mississippi Abbey, was newly founded when B.J. came along. Most of the sisters were young, and we spent our time planting and trimming Christmas trees, getting in the hay, and beginning our candy business, which kept us very busy along with our special vocation to pray for our confused world.

In 1974, this young man B.J. showed up and wanted to help us. We soon came to love and admire B.J. and his dog Blue, a huge Great Dane. B.J. had endured all the usual adolescent growing pains before he came to faith in Christ through his visit to our brother monastery a few miles away, New Melleray Abbey. I remember him sharing one story about his youthful days—one girlfriend had broken up with him and he had pretty much drowned his hurt in a bit of a drinking binge. He came home feeling utterly miserable, but his faithful dog Blue joined him on his bed and laid his head on him as if to say to his friend B.J. all will be well.

B.J. seemed to admire our cloistered life of simplicity, hard work, and prayer. We watched through those early years as this young man grew spiritually from a rough, impetuous youngster to a lover of Jesus. He would come out and help us get in the hay and he did all sorts of odds and ends and heavy lifting around our monastery. Gradually there seemed to grow within him a desire to save sinners (which we all are)—a deep, pure desire. From our cloistered hidden life, we watched B.J. grow like a miracle of grace. His youthful roughness had formed a man who was compassionate and understanding and able to touch those who suffered from their sins, as he had.

B.J. was also influenced and supported by the monks of New Melleray, its abbot Father Mathias, and the former hermit monk who became our chaplain, Father William Wilson. Mother Columba, our abbess at the time, also befriended B.J. and the two became fast friends. She provided the spiritual direction for his maturity and growth, as Father William provided scriptural teaching and discipleship.

B.J. finally met the love of his life, Sheila. We met her and I remember saying to B.J.—she is just like us (meaning us as Sisters dedicated to Christ). She was natural, no pretenses, generous, fun, loving, and the perfect partner for B.J. Poor Blue had to now accept second place. B.J. and Sheila visited our monastery through the years for important celebrations and anniversaries, and they come regularly for spiritual retreats. We are so grateful for having B.J. in our lives and watching him grow in his love for God.

Sister Lillian Shank grew up in Michigan and Ohio, graduated with a B.S. in Nursing from Mount St. Joseph's College, and worked in Cleveland, Ohio. She entered the Trappistine monastery in Wrentham, Massachusetts and was one of the 13 nuns who founded Our Lady of the Mississippi Abbey in 1964. Sister Lillian is currently living in a retirement community in Florida.

What a Mother Superior Learned from B.J. Weber

By Sister Gail, retired abbess

B.J. has been a friend of our community for almost 50 years. In a way, we have grown up together because when B.J. first came to our Abbey, we had only been founded for about six or seven years. In 2019, we are celebrating our 55th anniversary!

I learned most about B.J. from those he had reached out to in the name of Jesus Christ. Some would share their stories with us, stories of their deep gratitude to him for being the person through whom God saved their marriage, their sanity, their soul. B.J. is probably the only person I know personally whom I would call a real missionary of Jesus Christ today. Nothing is too trivial or big for him to put his heart into it.

One time when he had already been in New York a long time, we were working closely with Immigration to bring a young woman into the country to discern her calling to our abbey. B.J. was on vacation with Sheila and their family, but he took time to again give us good advice and put us in touch with people who could help. That was over and above the call of duty!

In about the year 1999, we were faced with a major fundraising project and we had NO experience, NO list of donors, and NO understanding of how to proceed.

I was Abbess at the time and I asked B.J. for advice since we knew he had lived "by faith" from support by individuals who cared about his ministry. He helped us out very generously. Besides advice, he gave us real people who were his friends and who could and would help us. B.J.'s constant mantra for me was: "Gail, you have to think out of the box!"

I learned a lot about trusting God and trusting other people from B.J. Even if people let him down or disappointed him, he had a faith in them—but ultimately faith in God.

B.J. thinks big, and doesn't hesitate to ask big—but he is grateful. He knows how to make people feel valued. He would use this skill with our sisters, and I could see that it really gave them a boost: to feel that someone thought they were important. They feel this way because, in fact, I believe B.J. really loves people with a genuine Christ-centered love. So if he is called on to help, he will be there. These are the qualities I admire most in B.J.: loyalty and total given-ness to Christ.

Sister Gail Fitzpatrick, a native of Fairfield, Connecticut, entered the Trappist/Cistercian Abbey of Mount Saint Mary in Wrentham, Massachusetts in 1956. She was one of the 13 Wrentham sisters who founded Our Lady of the Mississippi Abbey in Dubuque, Iowa in 1964, and she served as Abbess of Mississippi from 1982 to 2006.

The First Catholic Abbey in Norway Since the 13th Century

By Sister Kathleen

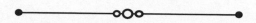

In 1999, after several years of prayer, exploration, and discussion, our Cistercian community outside Dubuque, Iowa, started a new monastery in Norway. Our Order (Order of Cistercians of the Strict Observance) had several monasteries there during the Middle Ages, but none for centuries now. The people of Norway were again ready to welcome the presence of Christian contemplatives in their land, especially as we were already part of their heritage.

We located land overlooking the ruins of our Order's 13th century monastery on the island of Tautra, which had been closed during a tragic and tumultuous era between Protestants and Catholics. Now the Lutheran Church of Norway and the Queen were welcoming us back with open arms.

We had enough sisters to send to start this new monastery, but construction in a first-world country is a very expensive proposition indeed. B.J. was supportive of the project all along, in many ways. As chief fundraiser, with zero experience, I often turned to him for advice and support. One thing which made a great impression on me was his willingness to share his donors with us—not a normal practice in the nonprofit world, where donors are often jealously guarded. That's the scarcity attitude. B.J. took an abundance attitude, that our God is a God of abundance. Because he was convinced that this new monastery was God's work, and a potential source of life for Norwegian Christianity, B.J. not only shared advice and supporters with us, but went to the trouble of bringing potential supporters to visit us.

We were thrilled when the Queen of Norway and the Archbishop of the Norwegian Lutheran Church attended the opening of our new abbey, Tautra Mariakloster, near Trondheim. Today the Queen, a Lutheran, has visited several times. Tour buses line up several times a day for hundreds of visitors to hear the ancient chants and prayers. All the while the growing community of Cistercian sisters in Norway keeps our traditions alive—a life of solitude and prayer—and maintain the ancient 7-times-per-day prayer services as well as their sustaining business of making handmade soaps.

Without B.J.'s friendship, fellowship, and networking, it would be safe to say we could not have built the monastery in Norway. He was the single most indispensable helper outside our own Order. For me it was an extra gift as I got to know B.J. much better, and as all his friends can say, our conversations always inspired and encouraged me, not only in the work, but more important, in my own faith in Christ.

Sister Kathleen O'Neill has been a Trappist nun at Mississippi Abbey (Dubuque, Iowa) for 40 years. A New Jersey native, she graduated from Bucknell University in Pennsylvania, and received a Master's degree in theology at the Catholic University of America in Washington, D.C

The Meals Friends Share

By a loyal hometown friend

I met B.J. at the age of thirteen. It was a difficult time for our family, as my sister was dying of cancer. Looking for a way to help, in an effort to relieve some of the pressure in the house, B.J. graciously invited me to live with him for the summer on the monastery farm. We stayed in a secluded farmhouse, which had broken windows, a slanting porch, and no running water or phone. It was healthful and robust living, and very rustic. We sweated and worked the farm during the day and at night we performed our ablutions in a spring-fed pond, the water getting colder the deeper you dared to sink. In the pond B.J. used only Ivory soap, "because it floated." He was full of homespun wisdom like that. In the evenings B.J. would make simple dinners—bratwurst, ham and cheese sandwiches, canned soup, more ham sandwiches—you get the idea. After two weeks B.J. cryptically implied he had to go do something, and instructed me to watch his dog, Blue. I thought "no problem." I liked Blue. B.J. left the house . . . and didn't return for three weeks. Three weeks! His absence to a 13-year-old was both confusing and liberating. Blue and I got along just fine, and

I retaliated against B.J.'s aloofness by trashing his beloved Chevy truck, a vehicle I didn't know how to drive, evidently.

When I turned 18, B.J. suggested I join him in his work in Times Square, at a place called the Lamb's. The Lamb's Mission attracted a randomly gathered network of kindred spirits, all united in their desire to serve God. (It was there I ended up meeting my wife of now 30 years.) Upon arrival, I summarily asked B.J. to show me to my room, as I expected another disappearing act from him and didn't want to be homeless. Oddly, this time he stuck around.

To indulge our midwestern appetites, we'd occasionally go to a place on 8th Avenue in Hell's Kitchen. The eponymous name of the joint was Jimmy Ray's. It was the quintessential dive bar, but the place had soul and they served great burgers. Also, it attracted the likes of Robert De Niro and Al Pacino, both frequent customers. One day I read a story in The New York Times, describing how the Health Department was fining violators of the Sanitary City Health Code. One of the top offenders was Jimmy Ray's. I showed the article to B.J. He read the story, smiled, and said it made him hungry. We went there that night for a burger, which we consumed with vigor. Sadly, a fire gutted Jimmy Ray's in 1987. A rumor took wing that Al Pacino's unpaid bar tab went up in flames.

B.J. and I continue to break bread, most often when he comes to Iowa to go on retreat at a monastery near where I live. He selects the night, either before or after his retreat. The unspoken

arrangement is simple: he provides the food and prepares the meal
while I clean up afterwards and pretend to laugh at his jokes. It's
a lot of work cleaning up after B.J.; he's a tsunami in the kitchen.
But his food is good and the arrangement works. At these meals we
talk about the characters woven into our collective past, our hopes
for the future, the books we're reading, how truth is revealed in
paradox, etc. Sometimes we'll share a moment of silence, generally
only broken when B.J. says something like, "Hey man, I love you.
Will you pass the salad?"

Through our meals and ensuing discourse, B.J. (whom I call
Beej) has taught me a lot about friendship, such as—it's okay
to be brutally honest. Once, when I was bereft at the breakup
with a girl singularly ill-suited for me, Beej and I took a walk.
As I was describing the pain of the loss, Beej pointed to a small
tree and said, "Listen, the chances of you marrying that girl are
about the same as you marrying that tree. Not going to happen,
so get over it." Another thing he taught me is that to keep a
friendship relevant requires agency and action. For instance, Beej
randomly calls just to check in, even though he's well aware of my
pathological aversion to the phone. When I repeatedly explain how
much I hate the phone he says something like, "I get it, I know.
I'll call you later and we'll talk about it." Lastly, one of the most
important lessons B.J. has taught me about friendship is this: just
show up, no matter how awkward or ridiculous it might seem or
feel like at the time. I've watched him do this on many occasions,
and he's right. It's a powerful testimony.

Writing these sentences is a little awkward for me, so I guess his prodigious influence is at work....

By a loyal hometown friend who still enjoys the companionship of the monks of New Melleray Abbey.

A Plato Scholar Surprised by "Adventures with B.J."

By Mark Moes, Ph.D.

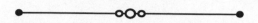

I clearly recall the morning I met B.J. in Dubuque, Iowa on my way to class at the ecumenical seminary there. I was a young man of 24, raised by Catholic parents, who had done an undergraduate degree in philosophy and classics at Notre Dame in Indiana, and who, like most college graduates of the 70s, had come under the impression (false, as I later learned) that it was my duty to reexamine the Christian faith for its epistemic credentials. I was doing an M.A. in theology in order to "consider the religious question."

It was early spring in the year of 1975, if I recall correctly. I was hitchhiking to class from my parents' home, only a few miles from the seminary, when an oversized Buick or Oldsmobile pulled up beside me with the head of a gargantuan blue Great Dane sticking out of the back-seat window. (Several years later, after Blue died, B.J. and I both were to take great solace from reading the Robinson Jeffers poem "The House Dog's Grave.") A sandy-haired B.J. asked me where I was going. To the seminary, said I. So am I, said he, and within minutes we were deep into a conversation about God, Incarnation, Atonement, girls, rugby, football, German lager beer, and the history of philosophy (did we discuss Tolkien during that ride? I believe we did). Instant friendship bonding occurred partly in spite of, but also partly because of, the fact that we had very different backgrounds. It was a case of an Oxford scholar meeting the musketeer D'Artagnan, and within fifteen minutes we had resolved not only to meet that evening at a workingman's pub in the old part of Dubuque, but also to fly to Denver together to watch an Old Boys' Rugby tournament. (B.J. was taking classes at the seminary as he was being discipled by several Trappist monks, but that is another story.)

Let me recall, from among hundreds of interesting stories that could be told about my adventures with B.J. during the mid-1970s, an incident from a philosophical theology class in which we were both enrolled that occurred just a few weeks after B.J. picked me up on the side of the road. Ralph Powell, a brilliant Dominican scholar who had read everything ever written in its original language, who was conversant with the whole history of philosophy and theology, who had been a personal friend of the Catholic "phenomenologist" Dietrich von Hildebrandt (the friend of Husserl whom Hitler had chased out of Austria, having commanded the SS to "bring me the head of Dietrich von Hildebrandt"), and who that day was reflecting about what were the crucial errors of Martin Heidegger's philosophy of Being, picked B.J. from among the dozen of us attending the class and posed him a question: *Do you think, Mr. Weber, that Heidegger's thought constitutes a real theism, or is it rather some form of covert pantheism?* I knew that B.J. did not have a strong academic background, and I was thinking to myself how I could save him by blurting out some question or comment that would divert Father Powell's attention to myself. B.J. never flinched. He apparently had been reading the second chapter of First Corinthians the day before with his mentor Father William Wilson. *"Father Powell,"* B.J. said, in a rough paraphrase of St. Paul, *"I don't think I understand Martin Heidegger at all. I don't come here with any greatness of words or of wisdom, but one thing I do know—Jesus Christ and Him crucified, and the spirit and the power that He makes available to us . . ."*

B.J. continued his paraphrase of 1 Corinthians 2 for a few lines, but I remember my heart racing within me and the feeling of joy elicited by his heartfelt evangel uttered in a context in which no one expected it. I had become accustomed to academic environments where intellect was sometimes divorced from heart and will. B.J. violated the customary expectations of the college classroom in a way that was not destructive but constructive (after all, this was a seminary classroom). Everybody loved it, including Father Powell.

I was at Oxford University in the Spring of 1979 when B.J. had just moved to the Lamb's Mission in NYC. In a letter (no texting or cell calls in those days) he invited me to stop in on him when I flew home to the States. On July 2, when I got out of the taxi from

LaGuardia at 130 W. 44th Street, a half block from Times Square, there was B.J. at the front door and we had a glad reunion after not seeing one another for seven months or so. He had somehow become community manager of the Lamb's and he showed me to my temporary "digs," which turned out to be the basement sauna rooms where everyone from Lionel Barrymore to Fred Astaire had sweated and showered. There is a lyric from Bob Dylan's song "Tangled Up in Blue" that expresses an aspect of what it felt like to live at the Lamb's that year: "I lived with them on Montague Street, in a basement down the stairs; there was music in the cafes at night, and revolution in the air."

The human traffic pouring in and out of the Lamb's Club in those days was amazing. Poets, playwrights, struggling musicians, street ministers, recovering (or still active) prostitutes and drug addicts and pimps all came in and out of those doors to see B.J. or one of us lay "ministers," or to get a meal at the free lunch that was offered. Late one night I came home to the Lamb's and standing in the lamplight by one of the front doors was (then) Carolyn Rossi deep in conversation with Paul Stuckey of Peter, Paul, and Mary fame.

Another day I was racing down the stairs in a hurry to meet someone I had kept waiting outside on 44th Street. In my haste I pushed myself between an old lady with grey hair done up in a bun and a younger man wearing an expensive suit. The two of them and a herd of other theatregoers were moving to the lobby for a drink during the intermission of a performance of "On Golden Pond" in the Off-Broadway theater on the third floor of the Lamb's. The lady with the grey bun was highly annoyed by my shoving. In a voice that was New England accent and somehow familiar she almost screamed: "Young man, you must be in a terrrrr-a-bull hurrr-ay." I turned around and apologized, pretending not to show my surprise when I recognized that I was speaking to Katherine Hepburn (who of course later performed in the film version of the play).

One evening (I can't remember if this happened in 1979 or a later year), B.J. and I were having a beer at the cozy little Oak Room bar just inside the front door of the Algonquin hotel down the street (once lunching place in the 1920s of Dorothy Parker and the Algonquin Round Table). We heard from the dining room someone playing beautiful renditions of old American standards. We peeked inside the dining room and there at the piano was a very young Harry Connick Jr. (he was unknown at the time, someone had to identify him for us).

Just as there are hundreds of interesting stories that could be told about my "adventures with B.J." during the mid-1970s, so there are hundreds of such stories about our adventures at the Lamb's as would-be street evangelists. Let me just recall one or two. Both have something to do with the reality of the demonic, the fallen created pure spirits. Some background is required to make these stories fully intelligible. In Dubuque, B.J. and I had both been friends of the evangelical Christian scholar Donald Bloesch. One night, B.J. and I had a meal with Bloesch at some bar and grill and were discussing theology (as we always did). I played the role of the secular intellectual and said to Bloesch something like, "Come on, Don, you can't really expect modern university-educated Americans to believe in a doctrine of atonement that has built into it a belief in devils, in Satan and evil spirits. The very mention of such things can only elicit laughter in a contemporary secular classroom." Bloesch looked at me seriously and said something like, "Then why do you consider yourself Christian? One thing I can tell you for sure—if Satan and the evil spirits are not absolutely and objectively real, then Christianity is false."

Fast forward to a dark October night in 1980. A full moon hung in the sky, periodically partly obscured by long wispy dark clouds. B.J. and I had resolved to do some street evangelism in Times Square that night, and we were walking west along 44th Street toward the Square. We were walking toward the full moon and about fifteen yards ahead of us limped along what looked to be a homeless man wearing dirty and decrepit clothing, an almost zombie-like figure. B.J. and I both felt stabs of compassion for this fellow, and we decided we would approach him with a word of love and an offer of free lunch or what have you. But when we sped up to catch up to him, before we had gotten within ten yards of him, he sensed us coming and spun himself around with a sudden agility, flexibility, and litheness that was quite startling (like Regan's head spinning around in the movie Exorcist). His horrifying face glared at us with what seemed like a supernatural hatred. One of his hands in mockery made the up and down motions of a priest waving the aspergillum to spread holy water on the congregation. And out of his mouth he shrieked, in a tone of mockery, hatred, and disgust, the words (B.J. and I both remember them exactly): "What do you want of meeeee, children of God?" (Later B.J. and I compared this guy to the chief soldier at the Gate of Mordor in *Lord of the Rings*, the one who "no longer knew his own name, but was known only as the mouth of Sauron.") B.J. and I drew back from this zombie in fear, for he was apparently, if not fully possessed, at least under the control of some hateful spirit. But we watched him for some time. A number of NYC cops "on the beat" avoided the guy, too, and he went around wailing something until he finally threw himself self-abusively into a metal trash basket. We never learned what became of him. But we did conclude that for "some like these, one fasts and prays at a distance."

Mark Moes received his doctorate in philosophy at the University of Notre Dame, his M.A. in philosophical theology at the Aquinas Institute, and B.A. from the University of Notre Dame. He is currently Associate Professor of Philosophy at Grand Valley State University in Michigan, specializing in Ancient Philosophy and teaching the close reading of Platonic dialogues. He has wide reading interests in Philosophy of History (Hegel, Collingwood, MacIntyre, etc.) and in Philosophy of Religion. He is the author of *Plato's Dialogue Form and the Care of the Soul* (Peter Lang, 2000), and a multitude of articles on ancient philosophy, philosophy of medicine, hermeneutics, metaphysics, epistemology, theology, Aristotle, and Plato and modern thinkers.

THE MONASTERY YEARS: A PHOTO ALBUM

B.J. baling hay at the monastery in 1977.

Sisters of Our Lady of the Mississippi Abbey (OLM) in 1970s.

B.J. helped the nuns with heavy lifting.

Father William Wilson during his hermit monk years.

Father William Wilson served OLM as chaplain, pictured with Abbess Mother Columba Guare.

Sisters of OLM in 2018. B.J.s friendship with them has lasted 45 years as he often brings guests for contemplative retreats. *Photo by Bill Witt.*

Mother Columba with B.J. months before his wedding.

Pictured in farm clothes, Abbott Father Mathias led B.J. to faith in Christ.

The Lamb's Club Street Mission and Church in Times Square

1979-1984

Times Square Shepherd Series, Part I

Ministering in the Street

Story by Elaine Johnson

Reprinted with permission from the July 29, 1979 Dubuque Telegraph Herald.

NEW YORK – A lanky black man has fallen unconscious across a sidewalk.

The Saturday night theater crowd parts to avoid him, some glancing down, most ignoring him as another piece of litter on the street already heaped with garbage.

A young minister in white pants and rolled-up sleeves finally kneels and slaps the man into consciousness. The face comes alive with a grimace of pain. The man seems to be crying silently, his head rolling uncontrollably from side to side. His skin carries the stench of sweat and filth and drunkenness; saliva dribbles down his chin.

The minister pulls the man to his feet and propels into the subway. They stop on an upper step where the man vomits into a corner as the minister tightens his grasp, his face set against the sight and smell.

A small group gathers to stare as the minister hauls the man to the Brooklyn stop. They watch as the man's legs bend under him and he pitches forward, his head thudding against the cement floor inches from the train track. Blood oozes from his nose.

A young black man calmly munches on a chocolate bar. "He's drunk. What're you doin' with him? He's drunk," he sneers. The minister is losing patience. "Look man, we're just trying to get him home."

He stoops and tucks a miniature version of St. John's Gospel in the drunk's pocket. Maybe he'd see it when he sobered up. He'd wonder how it got there, maybe he'd open it and see the name written there—"Pastor B.J. Weber"—and the address of the Lamb's Club mission.

Maybe he'd come in. But he'll probably become one of the many who don't.

Weber says his main responsibility "is not to be a harvester or to expect a harvest, but to plant seeds of conversion."

Pastor B.J. Weber is 32. He spent his youth roaming the quiet streets of Dubuque, although those thoroughfares were less quiet because of him.

Years later, he attended the University of Dubuque Theological Seminary while living and working at Our Lady of the Mississippi Abbey, a community of Trappistine nuns south of Dubuque. Weber prepared for his late-blooming ministry on the abbey's bluffs overlooking the Mississippi and vast stretches of farmland. Every week since January, Weber has worked at least four nights and into the morning at reclaiming souls against the backdrop of New York's decadent, populous Times Square area.

Junkies hawk drugs. Dead-eyed prostitutes line Eighth Avenue, the infamous Minnesota Strip. Street hustlers set up shop on corners to sell hot goods or collect bets. Derelicts and street bums sleep where they drop. The blaze of theater marquees promising sex, violence and horror keeps the streets alive into the early-morning hours.

This Times Square playground for the lewd, the deviant, the penniless, and the illegal is only a few blocks from the three-piece suits and the designer fashions of Madison Avenue. Peep shows and sex shops stand side-by-side with some of Broadway's proudest theaters. Hookers, junkies, and transvestites peddle their stuff in the shadow of the venerable New York Times.

During the six months Weber's been a self-support missionary with the Manhattan Church of the Nazarene, he has found a home, a church, and a way of life ministering to the street people who wash through the eight-block Times Square area.

"I love the opportunities to minister. I could be here forever," he says. "Each time I talk to people, it's like I get a rush of adrenaline. Part of it comes from wanting to defend myself physically and part comes when I realize that I'm doing this on faith—that Jesus wants me here, that God wants me here."

Weber's focus is "to be present and attentive. Those street people know exactly when you're not paying attention to them. When you spend time with them, they'll really respond.

"I don't view these people as different from me or different from Dubuquers because they're selling cocaine or because they're pimps or whatever. The media has robbed them of their personalities—of who they are—and has made them two-dimensional machines.

These are people, individuals who love and weep and cry. These people see that you look at them and are interested in them." There's Polly, an ageless baglady—jargon for the dozens of women who make their homes in the street, carrying all their possessions in shopping bags or plastic sacks.

Polly has claimed the stairs of an old off-Broadway theater as her home. She eats and sleeps there, as oblivious to the passing crowd as it is to her.

One minute, she is sensitive to a photographer's wandering lens.

The next, she is squatting in a corner of the theater steps, shielded by her stained white coat. She urinates into a plastic cup, tosses the contents into the 44th Street gutter and returns to her steps to prepare a meal of food scraps.

Weber greets Polly by name each time he passes. She responds with a puzzled face. Her brown eyes are curious, defensive; the mousy hair, a matted tangle of curls. Street gossips say she is the mother of grown children. But the street has been her home for years. She's built up a shell that Weber may never penetrate.

There's Jose, circulating through the crowded streets and hawking drugs. "Cocaine, try before you buy, cocaine, try before you buy." He offers Weber a sniff.

"Don't give me that jive. How come you selling dope? You're going to get in trouble. What if I was a cop, buddy? What would you do?" Jose turns his empty eyes to the sidewalk. "I'd go do some more time."

"Sure you would. You're going to get jammed up. We'll get you straight on that. We'll get you on a methadone program—you're on it—we'll get you off, we'll get you a job. Come visit me. Pastor B.J. right over at 130 W. 44th. Ask for me. I don't want to see you busted now."

Jose seems receptive. "B.J., I'll be over tomorrow." He never came.

A salami sandwich slathered with mayonnaise lies on the floor of a fast-food joint. Customers scuff around it until Ollie gingerly picks it up and takes it to a table. Weber is revolted.

"Look man, you can't eat that. Here, I'll buy you another sandwich." Pride makes the young man resist until Weber orders the sandwich for him. Ollie's face is full of gratitude.

Weber is preparing another tract. "Come and see me when you get straight. We'll help you out," he tells Ollie as he hands him the book.

"Yeah, I got a lot on my mind. I'll come." Later that night on the street, they cross paths again. Ollie is warm and receptive, as if greeting a friend, but he never shows up at the Lamb's Club.

Doria lounges on the hood of a parked car, spotlighted in the white pool of a streetlight. Fringed shorts and high-heels display her long legs. It is 2:30 a.m.—maybe she's waiting for a "john," someone to buy sex from her.

Weber exchanges a few words with her; he tells her that he wants to help her change her life through Christ.

"Isn't it a little late for that?" she asks. Her muscular arms, broad shoulders, and powerful body tell Weber she's already changed her life. She is a transsexual.

With every conversation, every friendly exchange, every passing day, Weber gains a stronger foothold among the area's regulars. After six trying months, he feels the tide is beginning to turn in his work. "Within the last couple of weeks, I feel the Lord has allowed me to make some real breakthroughs in the Times Square area. I'm just getting to the point where people are starting to recognize me. They see who I am, what I'm doing—they see that I'm not trying to jive them, not trying to rip them off.

"I'm trying to minister to their needs, to be present – to love them as Christ would love them. To share the gospel of Christ. Just recently some of the regulars are starting to recognize me and they trust me now."

Exposure to Times Square's endless landscape of human misery and moral blight has forged a change in Weber. "I'm less tolerant of sin, but I'm more compassionate to sinners. I know that sounds like a paradox, but I've got to be really non-compromised in everything I do.

"If anything, I'm more sensitive now. Part of the motivation is the satanic influence. I can never become thick-skinned. I must preach the gospel, bind up their wounds.

"When I first got here I thought all I had to do was lay it on people, but that's not what they need. They need compassion and love and someone who cares.

"God is changing their lives through my changing life. It's not by being as tough as they are or tougher than they are. It's by being gentle and kind and honest and showing them the love of God."

A Prodigal Past, A Caring Present

Story by Elaine Johnson

Reprinted with permission from the July 30, 1979 Dubuque Telegraph Herald.

NEW YORK – B.J. Weber went out six years ago to buy a loaf of bread. He found something else. His life was changed. Completely, simply, permanently.

He now believes God is compelling him to help others change their lives, too. Dressed in jeans and T-shirts or rolled-up sleeves, he makes the rounds of New York's seedy Times Square, praying over unconscious derelicts and talking about the love of Christ to the people who hustle, pimp, and peddle their bodies on the grimy streets of New York.

A strong faith sustains Weber in the face of constant human misery – a faith that has crisscrossed denominational boundaries, as Weber was raised a Lutheran, received spiritual guidance from a Catholic monk and nun, and graduated from a Presbyterian seminary before becoming a licensed pastor in the Manhattan

Church of the Nazarene.

The financial support of Dubuquers and other tri-state area church members also sustains Weber in his urban mission.

Dubuquers, who remember B.J. Weber as a troublemaker, a hard drinker, and a rugby player may have a difficult time picturing him ministering to the flow of humanity through the eight-block Times Square area.

Weber is a man who throws himself into anything with passion— from campus radical politics in the late '60s to the Dubuque Rugby Club he founded in 1970. Becoming a Christian and a minister hasn't changed his deep involvement in life, but has given it a new direction, meaning, and purpose.

"I'm not a bleeding heart," he says. "I see Christianity as a hardcore practical living. It's the greatest source of counseling, the greatest method of changed emotional problems. My life is a perfect example. I once was lost; now I'm found. I once was this person; now I'm different."

Weber, the son of Bill and Ginny Weber of 1100 Rhomberg Ave., talks about his former life with sheepish amusement. Although he's only 32, the scrapes and involvements of the first 26 years of his existence already are a lifetime away:

"He was a very colorful person for two years in high school," his mother recalls. "His name was in the News of Record almost every week. There were a lot of rinky-dink things. He fought a lot and was arrested for 17 speeding violations once and put in jail overnight. There were beer parties. B.J. was always the one who got caught. He was no angel—far from it. I guess he just about did everything."

As a student at Iowa State University in Ames, Weber was a leader of the student protest movement, a card-carrying Communist who chose to major in child development as a means of molding young minds in the spirit of communism.

College was also a time of promiscuous sex and experimentation with drugs. He isn't proud of that.

He was a traveler—or, as he recognizes it now, a searcher. He hitch-hiked to the Woodstock, N.Y., music festival, but he says he was so loaded with drugs he didn't know where he was. A carload of rednecks picked him up and shaved his head.

He went to Europe with his brother Mike, then moved to Southern California, where he sold used cars for a while. When Weber's rugby club was invited to compete in Jamaica, the team didn't go to the island, but he did and spent a month bumming around the warm beaches.

Although St. John's Lutheran Church in Dubuque played an active part in Weber's upbringing (his mother remembers him showing some interest in the ministry as a young teenager), he says his interest centered around the social activities of the church's Luther League.

Weber says the change in his life came when he "became a Christian" at 26. He describes it as "the point in your life when you accept Jesus Christ as Lord and God of your life. That means you decide to live a life according to the dictates of God." For Weber, the change was as dramatic and intense as the life that had gone before.

"I went out to New Melleray (a Trappist Monastery west of Dubuque) to buy a loaf of bread six or seven years ago. Father Mathias came up to me and said, 'Hey, you look interesting. What are you all about?' And I looked very suspiciously at him and started to question him and attack him about his pugilistic ties with the Catholic Church. He very patiently paid attention to me and took time to listen to me.

"Finally I asked him, 'Well, what're you all about?' And he told me a Christian who believes that Jesus is God; who changed his life and is changing his life through faith—'the assurance of things not seen.' I said, 'Hey, I want some of that.' So we prayed together and that was my spiritual birth."

Weber returned to New Melleray and met Rev. William Wilson, who was to become his spiritual mentor through the next five years.

Wilson recalls now, "He entered my life when he was on the threshold of making the greatest change in his life. He was taking God and Jesus with ultimate seriousness. B.J. is a man who lives intensely, so his embracing of Christian life had a difficult effect of separating him from what had gone before."

Weber's reputation as a man of excess seemed to carry over in his conversion experience. Wilson says, "His conversion was a spectacle before angels and men. It was a dramatic expression. "When God visited B.J., it was with psychological awareness—B.J. was aware of it. He was intensely attracted by religion, really drunk with the Lord. I watched this man and what God was doing in his life, but I was concerned how he was going to fare when God let his feet touch the ground again. Faith isn't just sustained by those highs."

Weber started making trips to New Melleray every day and his scripture studies soon took most of Wilson's time. "I tried to share my vision of God and Christian life. God was definitely using me as a means," Wilson says, emphasizing that Weber wasn't pressured to embrace the Roman Catholic faith.

The strength of Weber's new faith after his feet touched the ground convinced Wilson that the conversion was complete. "His faith had grown strong enough and deep enough. I knew that here was a man specially equipped for a life of permanent dedication.

"I sensed the conversion was real. B.J. was making a lifetime change. I sensed in the beginning with this man that God had very special plans for this man. God's given him a great ministry. B.J.'s never going to be ordinary. He has an extraordinary mission," says Wilson.

During B.J.'s conversion and his four years of study at the University of Dubuque Theological Seminary, he lived and worked at Our Lady of the Mississippi Abbey, a community of Trappistine nuns south of Dubuque. There, Abbess Mother Columba Guare served as Weber's spiritual director.

She says B.J. had a difficult time breaking with his former lifestyle. "Those were difficult years for B.J., filled with insecurity and uncertainty. For five years, he's really been through a lot of suffering. There have been great temptations and trials. It would have been easy for him to give up and go back to the old life." Ginny Weber credits the spiritual guidance of Guare and Wilson for keeping her son strong during those years. "I often think that Father William and Mother Columba knew more about B.J. during that time than we did. B.J. even calls Mother Columba his second mother. Maybe without them, he wouldn't have been able to do it."

Guare says Weber's major uncertainty of that period was in finding out what he was to do with his life. She and Wilson shared Weber's anxiety as his graduation grew closer.

"I saw this young man who had changed his life and had gone into the ministry and it wasn't clear in my mind what he would do. B.J. is the type—he just lives totally, he puts his whole self into whatever. He loves life and he loves people and he loves Jesus. Put those three together, and I knew he had to have something more challenging and exciting than a little country parish church someplace."

Direction finally came through Guare. She was mailed some information on a New York mission that served runaways. Weber made contact with the mission and was put in contact with the Lamb's Club, the mission of the Manhattan Church of the Nazarene. He joined the church last January as a missionary pastor responsible for raising his own financial support. Besides ministering to the area's street people, Weber is a "licensed pastor" of the Nazarene church, where he teaches a church Bible class and preaches at Wednesday evening services.

His street ministry originally worried his mother. "Four months ago," she says, "I didn't want any part of it. I used to worry. You're not aware of the evil that prevails in New York City until you have someone living there. I felt that he should have a church where I could go and hear him preach Sundays, but then I knew he'd never

be happy with that. He always needed a challenge—always."
Ginny Weber thinks her son's youthful ups and downs have given
him insights into his present ministry. "I think what B.J. went
through in his youth has helped to make him able to understand
everything that goes on in New York City."

She says she "wasn't surprised, but was really happy" when B.J.
announced his decision to become a minister. "He's a very outgoing
person. He has the ability to influence people and to win them
over. I remember his high school aptitude tests showed he would
make a terrific salesman. In a way that's what a minister is," she
says.

Ginny feels B.J. has an inborn ability to counsel and communicate
with others. "His brother and sisters think it's fantastic that he's
a minister. We all turn to B.J., we ask his advice. I don't have to
feel like he's my son. He has this charisma with people. No matter
who—he has something that makes them feel better."

Weber lives in a room at the Lamb's Club—a formerly famous off-
Broadway actor's club purchased by the Nazarene church in 1976—
and is supported completely by donations. Dubuque-area churches,
religious organizations, and private individuals who make monthly
commitments to Weber's support provide him with about $400 a
month in a city where the cost of living is 40 to 50 percent higher
than that of the Midwest. Weber sends monthly newsletters to his

supporters, which include the Trappistine convent and churches in Iowa.

There are detractors as well as supporters.

"I've heard, 'Well, why don't you come to Dubuque and work?'" says Weber. "I've said, 'Do you realize how many ministers and priests there are in Dubuque, Iowa? Do you know how many ministers and priests are working in the Times Square area? Two.' (Rev. Bruce Ritter, a Catholic priest, is the other street missionary.) The thing is this city spends lives. Just for the sake of gain, lives are tossed to and fro. You can just see the crushed people."

Ginny Weber acknowledges that some friends "still can't believe what he's done. They can't understand it. I just feel to understand what B.J. is doing you have to be a Christian."

Times Square Shepherd Series, Part III

Pastor B.J. Weber

By Elaine Johnson

Reprinted with permission from the August 2, 1979 Dubuque Telegraph Herald.

NEW YORK – It was very late the night of July 4 when Wanda's friends hauled her into the Lamb's Club. She collapsed in a lobby chair, almost dead of a heroin overdose. The medics had to cut her arm open to find a healthy vein for a transfusion.

As soon as Wanda was back on her feet, she forgot about the Lamb's and returned to the streets, shooting heroin into her tongue after the veins of her limbs collapsed under the needle's constant abuse.

Wanda is 18. She'll probably be dead within a month. She's one of the many who native Dubuquer B.J. Weber won't be able to save through his Times Square street ministry.

But Weber says the responsibility for Wanda lies with Christians all over, not just with the handful of urban missionaries scattered through a few cities.

"As far as the ministry, it shouldn't just be a person who's gone to seminary. It should be everyone's responsibility to do the works of the ministry.

"Whether you're in Dubuque, Iowa, or on the streets of Times Square, if you're separated from the love of Christ, you're hurting. Don't make things your god. If you really want to live a magnanimous life, let Jesus rule your heart with his love and give away what you are."

Six months after beginning his ministry, Weber feels he's found a home.

"Times Square is my church right now. I've got the biggest church in the world. The opportunities to minister are marvelous," he says. Weber says seeing lives changed by God gives him the greatest satisfaction in his ministry; his greatest grief comes when people turn their backs on the chance for change.

"It really grieves me when I talk to them about a changed life for Christ and what it means, and to see those people acknowledge that and accept it and then say, 'Hey, I'm not ready, that's good for you, but I got to eat.'"

In ministering to the runaways and street people of the Times Square area, Weber has observed that "most of the kids that run away and many of the street people have gotten in trouble because their parents haven't cared enough to discipline them, haven't cared enough to say no, to correct them, to be a model themselves. The parent has to be a living example of sobriety, of chastity, of moral living."

Weber says that one Iowa teen-aged runaway landed in New York and almost was led into prostitution by a pimp before the Lamb's Club sent the girl back with her parents.

At the heart of Weber's ministry is the belief that the church must combine an uncompromising doctrine with social action. It's a challenge he offers all church members.

"Christianity has always been formulated to be not a religion of ministers and priests, but a religion of the people doing the works of the ministry. Pastors, teachers are not to be out raising funds and doing administration work, they're supposed to be preaching and teaching the word of God to edify the saints so that they will do the works of the ministry."

In looking to the future, Weber says he may be in Manhattan forever or, "if the Lord provides us, we expand into other big cities."

Weber also looks forward to seeing the Manhattan Church of the Nazarene, his current church, open a sexual victims counseling service on the other side of Times Square. Working with him in the expansion of his ministry is another Dubuquer, Mark Moes, who arrived in Times Square in July and plans to stay at least a year. Moes, a graduate of the Aquinas Institute of Theology in Dubuque, recently completed a year of study in England. "I know this is where I'm supposed to be right now," he says. "I've been praying about this all spring and the guidance has been fairly clear." Although Weber's work consists mainly of "planting seeds of love and conversation in the hostile environment of Times Square," he says he doesn't live in fear of the violence that is a way of life there. He has had brushes with danger: his life was threatened by the Iowa girl's would-be pimp when he sent her home to her parents, and he acknowledges feeling a surge of adrenaline—of wanting to protect himself—during each street encounter.

Beyond the inevitable danger of Weber's work is the frustration involved in the slow labor of trying to change lives and in the constant exposure to the world of conventional success and material comfort he's turned his back on. But he says he doesn't expect that frustration to lead him from the ministry he's chosen. "I will stay. Whatever hardships I happen to be under, I will stay because I see that it's not just projects, it's not social work, it's not just money that makes a difference. It's a person's presence, a person sharing Christ here that makes a difference. You can give all the money away to a person, but unless they see their own spiritual wasteland—that they need to be filled with God's love—they're never going to change.

"It's only through conversation that people will change."

The Immigrant Who Gave Back

By William Gadea

It was May of 1979 when I arrived from Nicaragua at The Lamb's Mission & Church in Times Square on Mother's Day. I was basically homeless with no place to live, no money, and no one to help me. I was provided with a place to stay for the night at the Lamb's Church of the Nazarene by the Reverend Paul Moore and his family.

The next day, I met B.J., who without hesitation offered me a warm welcome and organized my permanent stay at the Lamb's. After a few days, he helped me register at English American Institute where he agreed to pay for my English grammar classes. There were some legal documents that needed to be signed. B.J. without question signed the documents. He became my legal guardian. The process of changing my tourist visa in America to a student visa was completed through B.J.'s generosity and belief in my potential to become the person I have become today. I was able to attend Eastern Nazarene College on a soccer scholarship and the President's Scholarship, because B.J.

encouraged me to practice soccer every day in Central Park. In addition, B.J. was instrumental in obtaining the additional funding for my tuition through the generosity of the Church of the Nazarene's members, as well as friends of B.J.'s in Iowa and other parts of the country.

In May of 1985, I received my Bachelor of Science degree in Pre-Med/Chemistry. Subsequently, I went to graduate school at the University of Massachusetts for a Master's in Medicinal Chemistry. I continued my education pursuing a Physician Assistant degree from Long Island University. I graduated in September of 1991. Dr. Susan Winchester, who was my professor in PA school, and her to-become husband, Father William, were both friends of B.J. Both of these people motivated me to persevere in my dream of becoming a medical provider.

I did three years of cardiothoracic surgery training as a physician assistant at Boston University Medical Center. My third degree was a Master's in Hospital Administration from Southern New Hampshire University.

Every achievement and goal completed in my life I owe to B.J.'s generosity and the people who contributed to B.J.'s request to help support my education.

Thanks to B.J., I have been able to provide generous medical care in third world countries and places where cardiac surgery is not available.

I always make sure to keep B.J. informed of the work I am doing, whether it is in Vladivostok, Russia, Seoul, Korea, Tanzania, Africa, Cochabamba, Bolivia, Managua, Nicaragua, or Guam. The credit goes to B.J. for believing in my dream of becoming a medical provider.

I will always be grateful for B.J.'s unconditional kindness and generosity.

William E. Gadea, PA-C, MSM, is the Chief of Physician Assistants at the David Grant Medical Center Heart, Lung & Vascular Center, at Travis Air Force Base.

Involuntary Fellow Traveler

By David Grizzle

B.J. Weber has been called by God to serve the poor of New York City streets and Bolivian villages, and also the wealthy executives and politically powerful from all over the world. I once aspired to be one of the very wealthy and powerful to whom B.J. was called. Looking back, I only succeeded at being a moderately wealthy executive and completely failed at my calling to be politically powerful. Despite my shortcomings and general failure to meet the admission requirements to enter his penumbra, B.J. let me be a beneficiary of and participant in his ministry anyway.

I did not necessarily seek the participation role.

When I first met B.J. in my mid-twenties, I would have been content to be one of the adoring baby bankers and lawyers who met with him early on Tuesday morning each week in Times Square to hear, but not experience, what B.J. had done the night before. I was actually accomplished at expressing admiration for what B.J. was doing when my principal feeling was gratitude that it was he and not I who had been out all night on the street meeting dirty people. I was completely fulfilled to hear, but not touch.

But B.J. could not leave good enough alone.

One morning when all the little suits had gathered at the Lamb's waiting for B.J., he came in late with a guy right out of Superfly central casting—a big, tall black guy with a long leather coat and a white wide-brimmed hat. B.J. explained that this was Alphonso and without reservation or embellishment explained that Alphonso was a pimp in Times Square who had just given his life to Jesus. Alphonso proceeded to sit down among us suits as if he were also among the future wealthy and powerful. (One of my concerns was that, since I had already begun to see my own limitations, I feared that Alphonso might actually fulfill the admission requirements to B.J.'s penumbra before I did.) I proceeded to network.

"Alphonso," I earnestly inquired, "How did you happen to give your life to Jesus? I'm just so curious about the path your life has taken to this glorious point. Did you have a long-standing interest in Christianity?"

"No, man. I didn't know sh*t about no Christianity," Alphonso responded.

"Thank you for explaining that, Alphonso. I'm just so very interested then in how you found yourself in a position to be receptive to B.J.'s invitation to give your life to Christ. Were there other people along the way who had caused you to think about God?"

"Oh, yeah, man. You know those guys with those beanie caps with tables set up on the sidewalk selling oils and other sh*t?" Alphonso explained as he began to unpack his salvation story.

"I think they are men of the Muslim faith," I added, hoping to draw him out further.

"I don't know what the f**k they is, man, but anyways, I was talking to one of them and asked why they out selling all this sh*t and he say it's 'cause God tolds them to and I say, 'How you knows God told you?' and he say, ''Cause I knows God,' and I say, 'How's you know God?' and he say, ''Cause I lives with God.'"

"Now, he had my attention," Alphonso editorialized. "So, I say to him, 'If you lives with God, then where do God live?' 'He lives in Flatbush,' he say."

"At that moment, I did not knows a lot about God, but I knows God don't live in no Flatbush. And then I meets B.J."

"Well," I thought to myself, "That's certainly an inspiring and unusual coming-to-faith story."

Little did I know that in the whole of the next forty years of my life with B.J., Alphonso would only be the very tiny tip of a very large iceberg of the unusual.

Editor's Note: After B.J. met Alphonso on the streets of Times Square— leading him to repentance and forgiveness through faith in Christ— Alphonso sold his drugs and paid off his girls. Then B.J. sent him to live with friends in Ohio, where an entire church adopted him as their own and gave him work in a painting company. Alphonso settled into an honest life and sincere pursuit of Jesus. For those who are skeptics or struggle with suspicion, our Ohio friends exemplified the true work of the church in the world.

David Grizzle (Harvard B.A., J.D.) is founder of Dazzle Partners, LLC, served as Senior Vice President of Continental Airlines, and as Chief Operating Officer and Acting Deputy Administrator for the Federal Aviation Administration (FAA). He and his wife Anne co-chair World Vision's campaign to raise $1 billion to combat extreme poverty across the globe.

"How Do You Solve a Problem Like Dear B.J.? How Do You Hold a Moonbeam in Your Hand?" (Sound of Music)

By Carolyn Rossi Copeland

The way I remember it, B.J. arrived at the door of the Lamb's where I was the first person to greet him. He had on a blue and grey rugby shirt. He carried a duffle bag with leather straps. He was straight from Iowa and the Monastery and he told me he was here to serve the poor. O.K. sure, why not?

We were starting all kinds of ministries at the Lamb's. Have a dream, have a calling, step right up. Paul Moore, the senior pastor, was all about building a midtown mission to the poor, to actors, to prostitutes, to drug addicts, to the homeless. B.J. found his niche and we became solid friends. I was schooled in convent schools, so I was not afraid of his practice of Christianity and habit of ending every prayer with "Alleluia, Amen."

The years moved swiftly. We witnessed each other's marriages, children, parents' deaths, and children's weddings. We are now grandparents. There are many stories I could tell to celebrate his 40 years in NYC, and I have chosen the one which illustrates how God used him to save the life of one orphan from Siberia.

Our small Hudson River town of Garrison was home to an adoption agency that focused on Russian Orphans. Helen, our Belarussian nanny, was now working part-time to help assist in the logistics of these adoptions. In the summers the agency brought about 15 young children to our town, where the children would perform in their native costumes and hopefully connect with families seeking adoption.

My husband and I hosted several of these children and were trying to find them homes. By the end of the three weeks, certainly all the girls were adopted and most of the smaller boys. We were heart-broken that Toli, the little boy staying with us, was not adopted. He was very loving but had learning issues. As he boarded the bus to leave, my husband and I committed to finding him parents or we would adopt him. We had 4 young daughters.

What we believed was an answer to prayer was that a friend of ours began the adoption process for Toli and Misha, another boy from the orphanage. They visited the boys in Siberia several times. They began sending money to the orphanage to support Toli and Misha. We were confident Toli would have a family and the bonus of a brother from the orphanage.

It was not meant to be. Toli was not adopted. Our friends, because of personal reasons, were only able to adopt one of the boys. Our hearts were broken for Toli, who believed he was leaving Siberia, but was left behind in the overcrowded orphanage. My husband and I revisited the idea of adopting him.

We called B.J. to talk, to pray, and to hear his wise counsel. He immediately said, "I'm going to write about Toli in my newsletter and let's see if we can find him a home."

We waited and prayed. B.J. heard from an interested family. A couple whose daughters were in college wrote that they were seeking God's direction for their next adventure. B.J. told them about Toli and the orphanage. He told them about Toli's learning difficulties. He encouraged them to go to Siberia to visit the orphanage. That trip happened and when the couple returned to the U.S., they told B.J. that they would be adopting Toli, and they felt led to adopt another boy, Toli's close friend from the same orphanage. This family would add two boys to their two daughters. We all rejoiced that these two young boys were given the gift of a loving mom, dad, and sisters. B.J. was willing to put forth the need to his network, a fellowship of men and women who know him, trust his discernment, and are willing to answer the call of loving each other.

I have been on the other end of the phone when B.J. is seeking to help someone in need. I take his calls seriously. B.J. has lived the scriptures—reaching out to the least of these, the widows, the orphans, the prisoners, and the tax collectors. He has entertained the rich, the powerful, and the meek and lowly, all with the same measure of generosity. The ripple of acts of obedience stretch beyond the visible. When B.J. is called home, he will certainly be greeted with "Well done, my good and faithful servant."

Carolyn Rossi Copeland founded the award-winning Lamb's Theatre in 1978 (sold in 2006). She was VP of Creative Affairs for Radio City Entertainment/Madison Square Garden. She has thirty years' experience producing more than 50 Off-Broadway plays and musicals, most recently "Freud's Last Session," and the Broadway musical "Amazing Grace."

"What were you thinking?"

By Sheila Meeder Weber

The first time I met B.J., who has been my one and only husband since 1980, it was a shocking experience. He was brash, boisterous, burly, and uncommonly emotionally inquisitive (alright, some would say invasive). But, he made me laugh so hard that first night amidst a group where he "held court" that my face hurt the next day.

I had been in New York City working as an assistant editor at *McCall's* magazine. In 1977 when I arrived, New York was a dangerous and dirty town. It had been on the verge of bankruptcy for several years. There were homeless folks living on the streets, and thieves would grab the gold chain right off your neck as you were walking down the street in broad daylight. I dared not take the subway after 7 p.m. when the rush hour crowd was starting to die down. Central Park had no grass and was full of rats.

Drug traffickers and prostitutes were right out on the street where you would pass them, with resulting threat of theft and violence, whereas today much of this activity is hidden by the internet. Certain neighborhoods were more dangerous than others—Times Square, Harlem, and the Lower East Side were among the worst. Peep shows and X-rated movie houses stood where today there are Disney shows, Madame Tussaud's, stylish bistros, and flowered plazas. No matter what your politics, I give credit to Mayor Giuliani, who as NY Attorney General closed the porn shops, and as mayor brought the sparkle back to The Big Apple. He changed this city so drastically that I always say Mayor Guiliani changed my life. Why? Because later, my own children by 6th grade could come home from school safely by themselves, which never could have happened in the 1970s.

In the spring of 1979, my parents came to visit me and wanted to see the mission church in Times Square they had heard so much about, called the Lamb's Club (officially the Lamb's Manhattan Church of the Nazarene—it also housed the Lamb's Theater.) I had just returned that very week from Israel where I had a small role in a movie called the JESUS Film, so that I could promote the movie on its national media tour. (Now the most widely viewed film in history, translated in more than 1400 languages and dialects!) My friend Jean Nolting worked at the Lamb's, so she planned our tour for the Saturday after Easter, April 21, 1979. We kept waiting for a guy named B.J. who Jean had arranged to give us the tour, but he was so late that we had other folks show us around the building. Then a group of 12 of us went next door to the China Bowl to have dinner. Finally, B.J. rushed into the restaurant, wearing rugby shorts and all covered with mud. He huffed and puffed and said, "I'm sorry . . . the game was late and the subway was late." Then he looked down the table, caught my eye, and said, "I'll get a shower and be right back." I later learned that Jean had arranged this blind date set-up— B.J. knew it, but I didn't. He told me later that he wanted to check out whether this set-up was going to be worth his time.

Quick as a flash he was back in a few minutes. The only seat available was across the table from my mom and dad, from whom B.J. learned my entire life history in the next two hours. So his first date with me was really with my parents. At the end of the meal, B.J. asked everyone to open their fortune cookie and read the tiny paper to the group. He was the last and said "Eureka, today is your lucky day. You are going to meet a beautiful young woman who works for *McCall's* magazine." At which point I turned beet red and wanted to crawl under the table. My sweet-as-sugar mom naively asked, "Does it really say that?"

My mom also happened to drop the fact that I was "practically engaged." (But my mom was wishfully overstating; she didn't know that we were about to break up.) To which B.J. replied, "Well, I don't see a ring on her finger, so if that guy is dumb enough not to put a ring on her finger, then she is fair game to me." So glad I didn't hear that conversation at the time.

A smaller group of us went elsewhere for dessert, where B.J. told every funny story he knew and my cheeks were starting to hurt from laughing so much. I was not initially attracted to him in the boyfriend kind of way; I just thought he was quite a character . . . and quite full of himself. In the middle of his "routine" where no one really could get a word in edgewise, he leaned over to me and whispered, "What's the matter, cat got your tongue?!" He was venturing to the edge of being irritating. Or captivating. I couldn't quite figure it out just then.

As we walked back to the Lamb's, I asked him how he approaches the homeless, runaways, or prostitutes on the street to get their attention so that he could intervene to get them help. "Oh, I just say . . . h-e-y, b-a-b-y!" he smirked in a flirty fashion. I was appalled and looked it. So when he said to me, "Has anyone ever told you how beautiful you are?", I had pretty much reached my limit with his astounding over-confidence and found myself thinking, "Buddy . . . you need someone to put you in your place." So I said with slight derision, "Yes, as a matter of fact they have." Aha, he thought, she's a contender . . . perfect!

He asked for my phone number in front of my father, so no fiddling with the digits. The rest is history and more to tell at a later time, but it was sort of like jumping off a cliff to marry a street minister who had no money. Back then folks would ask me quite frequently, *How could you marry him and live for five years in a street mission in Times Square?* And how did my parents feel about it? Here is the window into that answer.

My father was a United Methodist minister in Washington, D.C. and my mother was a fourth-grade public school teacher in the Stevens School four blocks from the White House. For this reason, inner city living was not new to me, and I understood the calling which brought a lifestyle of service to the needy.

My dad had been heavily involved in the civil rights movement and the anti-war movement of the 1960s. As a teenager, I had a front row seat. I have a devastating memory of our household getting a phone call on April 4, 1968, before any media reports came out, from one of my dad's best friends, Dr. James Laue. He called to share the overwhelming news with us that he was the first person to find Martin Luther King Jr. on that fateful Memphis balcony. Having rushed out from his hotel room when he heard the shot, our friend is pictured in those iconic *Life magazine* photos as he cradled Martin Luther King Jr. in his lap with hotel towels. Jim had been a member of my dad's former church, had been traveling with King's team, and in his own state of shock, was calling for comfort and pastoral care. Over the next few weeks, our parsonage townhouse at 20th and H Street was caught in the middle of a city aflame with violence and riots. The danger was real, yet somehow my dad thought it worthwhile to take me, age 13, along with him into the burned-out sections of D.C. to deliver food and clothing.

At other more peaceful times, my dad created multiple ways to teach me life lessons in the incubator of his inner-city pastor's world. My dad took me to St. Elizabeths Hospital where he played the piano and I sang to connect with people who were struggling with all sorts of mental illness. My parents also taught me how to set a proper table, serve and clear the plates, and "waitress" in our clergy home when we had formal events and even an occasional U.S. Senator for dinner.

I share these stories about my D.C. teenage years because I think it's important context that shows how all along God was preparing me for ministry in New York City.

Another facet of my preparation was coming to personal faith in Christ. I had a few teenage years where I rejected Christianity entirely by claiming that it was intellectually untenable for me—really just a smokescreen for the fact that I wanted to do what I wanted to do. Finally, three of my close college friends created a great disturbance in me by coming to my dorm room and alerting me that they had just attended a special event where they made a first-time decision to follow Jesus. I did not like hearing the news and was still heavily resistant. Eventually they dragged me along to a weekend retreat where I tearfully turned my mind, soul, and will back over to the Lord. It was a homecoming of my heart.

Now as a Christian with a background in inner-city ministry, all God had to do was get me from my native D.C. up to New York

City. How He did that is also a miraculous story worth telling. When Jimmy Carter won the Presidency, the Carters made big news by putting their daughter Amy in public school. Remarkably, and now I say providentially, my mother Verona Meeder was the fourth-grade teacher who became Amy's teacher. We still have a thick stack of news clippings from the overwhelming coverage my mom received in between the time the Carters made the announcement to when Amy entered the classroom. My mom was on *CBS Evening News* with Walter Cronkite, *Good Morning America*, and the list goes on. The news coverage was blocked once Amy became a student, but *McCall's* magazine contacted my mom and the school to ask if they could run an end-of-school feature on Amy's public school experience.

I was a senior journalism student about to graduate and had already freelanced a lot of stories for D.C. suburban newspapers, so I asked my mom if she would inquire with *McCall's* whether they would let me write the story. (I don't know what got into me . . . nothing ventured, nothing gained, I suppose.) The *McCall's* editor said I could send them something and they would pay me $500, and then re-interview my mom and heavily tweak the story the way they wanted. They also said that the story had to be ghost-written, citing my mom as the author. So I became a fly on the wall in her classroom and went on a class field trip or two. I sweated bullets on that story. *McCall's* ended up loving it, changing only a few sentences, and paid me the going rate for freelance writers of $1,250! I explained to their editor that I was graduating and leaving my U.S. Senate job (the Senator was soon retiring) where I had written every press release, newsletter to constituents, and the Senator's home-state newspaper column for the last year. *McCall's* offered me a paid summer internship which turned into a full-time job. I only planned to stay in New York for one year. As I write in 2019, it has now been 42 years!

A fun story from this time period was the day Rosalyn Carter took our family on a private tour of their White House living quarters. We got to see the Lincoln Bedroom, and she pulled "Jimma" out of a Cabinet meeting to meet us, where standing in the Rose Garden, he said to my mom, "If Amy gives you any problems, you just call me." That brought a big chuckle from my younger brothers. We gave Amy a Springer Spaniel puppy (named him Grits!) that our dog had fortuitously delivered on election night—the photo of Amy and our puppy landed on the cover of *Time Magazine*, titled "The Carters Move In." The President and First Lady were extremely kind, genuine, and down-to-earth, as they have always been known to be.

So there you have it. If the Carters had not moved into the White House and placed Amy in public school, I may not have found myself in New York City where I met the larger-than-life B.J. Weber!

From my wonderful husband, I have learned more lessons than all the ones cumulatively contained in the stories here.

There are so many stories that will never be told—in fact, stories that sometimes I didn't even know happened until some random accidental occurrence. There was an older single mom on public assistance who regularly sat out on her stoop down our block; she later thanked me for the window air conditioner that my husband had bought her when the temperature hit 102 and she had no relief. I didn't even know. Then 15 years later her son knocked on our door asking if B.J. would lead his mom's funeral. That is when I finally learned that B.J. had intervened to help counsel this fatherless man when he was a teenager getting in serious trouble—the young man now leads a thriving adult life, married and employed. So B.J. went to the mom's funeral and was at first greeted with threatening and skeptical glances by every person there (it was in Harlem and a bit out of B.J.'s cultural context) until he was able to share the sermon. Then two cops in the audience said, "Hey Rev, really nice job. We think we should give you a ride home in our police car."

Then there is Craig, a prisoner serving two life sentences for capital crimes. B.J. first went to visit him in prison some 20 years ago because one of our friends had gone to high school with Craig and asked that B.J. provide some pastoral care. Over the last 20 years, B.J. and a host of New York Fellowship interns have regularly traveled out to the New Jersey maximum security prison to visit Craig. These visits led Craig to personal faith in Christ, and he became an avid student of the Bible. Craig still holds little prospect of getting out of jail anytime soon, but for many years he has led Bible studies with other prisoners and offers a ministry of redemption and spiritual restoration behind the prison walls.

Another poignant story was Lublin, the U.N. ambassador from Albania, who was diagnosed with life-threatening cancer. He and his wife came from an Islamic background, but largely in name only, because that was the predominant culture of their country. Lublin originally met B.J. in a small ambassadors' luncheon that B.J. hosted twice a month to discuss the "teachings of Jesus," to which the marvelous female ambassador from Israel also attended (that is yet another story—how we grew in deep friendship with her and her husband during her two year assignment to the U.N.). We hosted Lublin and his wife for dinner in our home many times. Later, B.J. sat by Lublin's bedside as he lay dying, and despite Lublin's heritage, he asked B.J. if he would lead a Christian funeral for him, which B.J. led at both the U.N. Chapel and at the burial in Queens, NY.

As with so many of you, there are more stories than can ever be told. But as we share some of them, we can learn from each other. From my own husband, I have learned lessons about generosity of spirit, caring for those who seem forgotten, offering grace to others instead of judgment, resting in the love of Christ, trusting Him with our earthly affairs, and believing in His redeeming grace at work in our hearts, with prayers for God's prevenient grace at work in the world.

Sheila Weber has been married to B.J. since August 2, 1980. In addition to being Executive VP of the New York Fellowship—serving its non-profit management needs, offering hospitality, and managing the ministry house—Sheila has had more than 25 years' experience in public relations and as media spokesperson on more than 500 radio and TV broadcasts, most recently spearheading The Bible Literacy Project (first textbook for academic study of the Bible in public schools, now in 45 states and 650 high schools), and also founding National Marriage Week USA (Feb. 7-14). Sheila and B.J. raised their son Max and daughter Rachel in midtown Manhattan—both of whom are now married with children of their own, resulting in B.J. and Sheila becoming completely besotted with their (currently) five grandchildren, ages 6 months to 6 years.

B.J. the Braveheart

By Jamie Copeland

My wife and I can take some credit for B.J. leaving the job of Associate Pastor of the Lamb's Manhattan Church of the Nazarene. It was at the time of my father-in-law's death in 1987. B.J. and Sheila had invited Carolyn and I for dinner at their apartment in the church building. Out of deference to my wife's Italian roots, they served us wine with the meal, even though the Nazarene denomination is strictly opposed to the consumption of alcohol. As fate would have it, the Senior Pastor's wife stopped by just as the wine was being dispensed.

The church really wanted B.J. to stay, but he would have to sign a document saying he would not drink beer or wine. Alas, God obviously had another plan for Brother B.J. Sometime later, B.J. informed me that he had landed a new position as President of the New York Fellowship. *Wow, I thought, just a few months ago he was a minister to prostitutes and the homeless in Times Square and now he is the president of some organization.*

This, I thought, was too good to be true. I pressed him for more details. He ultimately revealed that he was this new firm's only employee. When I pressed him further for a description of what he actually did for this organization, he said, and I quote, "I am available to people." End quote.

Of course, it is a God thing. Who else could come up with a job description like that? It has inspired his Christian siblings to seek a closer walk and a bolder life. At some point, B.J.'s availability has blessed us all.

B.J. and I both have daughters. As their relationships with men became more serious, I sought out B.J.'s good counsel on what to say to potential suitors, should I have the opportunity to speak with them in private about their intentions. He suggested two somewhat interchangeable and visually memorable admonishments for me to use to set a proper tone for the Father-to-Boyfriend relationship. The first directive went something like this: "You break her heart, I break your legs." His second, slightly more graphic notification went thusly: "You wrong my daughter and I will drown you in a pool of your own blood."

While I have never had to use either of these forecasts, B.J. has provided me with a model of boldness in counseling young men on the timelessness of chivalry and a closer walk with Christ.

James Masson Copeland is an architect and
founder of the award-winning Hudson Design,
a company offering architecture, planning,
construction management, and interior design
services, based in Garrison, NY.

Rugby and Miracles

By Peter Hawkins

I was living in Los Angeles and I was a bit chewed up from playing rugby. I vividly remember the day I went to a healing service at the Anaheim Convention Center. My prayer on the healing line was, "Jesus, if you're real, today would be a great day to let me know." That prayer was answered profoundly, and the healing of my injuries was only just the beginning.

Soon after that service and with a baby on the way, my wife and I headed back East. I started a new investment company in New York City and began making calls. One morning I had three appointments. At the first, I was talking about interest rates and happened to mention rugby. The client said, "I know a rugby guy: B.J. Weber. He's a minister. Do you know him?" At my second meeting, the same thing happened. "Rugby? Do you know B.J. Weber?" My third meeting was with the Reverend Ken Swanson. "You must meet B.J. Weber," he told me. Three appointments, and all three people bring up B.J. I asked Ken where I could find this B.J., and I went straight to the Lamb's Club in Times Square. B.J.

answered the door. We talked for hours and became dear friends. B.J. and Sheila soon came to visit us in Connecticut. Our son was now born, and they wanted to see what it was like to have a child. Fortunately for Max and Rachel, the visit went very well! Over the years we started a sevens rugby team, there were events at the Lamb's Club and at the Webers' townhouse, and our son Simon went on a mission trip to Bolivia with Sheila and B.J.

At B.J.'s 50th birthday celebration, I was offered a ride home by the late Jim Ford who invited me to a men's prayer group started by B.J. and a few of his friends. It was eight guys at the time. With me and a few other new participants, the assemblage skyrocketed to twelve—a 50% growth rate. Today the group is known as the New Canaan Society and has 20,000 members worldwide.

My involvement with the New Canaan Society put me in touch with powerful prayer partners. This became especially important in 1999 when my family was involved in a fight against our son's prep school where boys were being sexually molested. The school tried to bury the issue and destroy our son who brought the situation to light. Twelve NCS guys prayed alongside me every single week for seven years. I called them 'The Dirty Dozen' because they were willing to get dirty on their knees and pray.

It may have taken seven long years, but the ramifications were staggering in the end. The school plead guilty in criminal court and issued 25,000 letters apologizing to our son. The extensive, international press coverage shed light on sexual abuse at prep schools and opened the door for victims in other schools to come forward. We soon found ourselves on the front lines offering guidance to others. Besides exposing abuse at many other schools, our fight led to groundbreaking decisions in the New Jersey and Massachusetts Supreme Courts as well as the United States Supreme Court, and a Pulitzer Prize for a *Wall Street Journal* reporter.

I give so much credit to the power of prayer and the support of 'The Dirty Dozen' for this victory. And all this would not have happened without B.J. and the New Canaan Society. My family and I will be forever grateful to B.J., and since Sheila is the rock and wise counsel behind this great man, we are forever grateful to her, too. The extraordinary part is that this is but one world-altering story in an epic of so very many good deeds done by the Reverend B.J. Weber. May he never stop!

Peter Hawkins is a financial planner and broker with United Planners Financial Services of America and based in Darien, CT.

The Ripple Effects

By Daryl Murray

I was an impressionable teenager in the early 1980s when I first met B.J. I was in the youth choir at my church and we were visiting the Lamb's Church of the Nazarene as one of our stops along the way. B.J. was telling us about the church, when in the middle of his orientation he asked the question "What are you doing?" It took me a moment to realize he was directing the question to me. I had no idea what he meant by "What are you doing," and why he had singled me out in front of my peers. He said something like, "We don't do that here!" I still had no idea what he was talking about. After a moment of explanation, it was pointed out to me that I had my arm around a fellow female youth group member and B.J. was "calling me out." I'm sure I was a little embarrassed to be singled out like that. After observing B.J. over the years, I came to learn that he often says things to evoke a "shock value" to the hearer. He has a way of getting people's attention. As I have gotten to know and love B.J., I have tried to hide or suppress any surprise by what he says. Instead, I try to respond with my own deflecting comments so as not to be disarmed by his provoking remarks. Although, I must admit, he often challenges my status quo thinking.

Over the next few years, B.J. visited our church, and our youth group made return trips to NYC where I was further exposed to a much harsher reality, one that challenged the "holy huddle, Christian bubble" in which I lived and was quite comfortable. The persona of The City itself had its own effect on me, and B.J.'s more radical version of his faith evoked a further evaluation of my own. Fast forward a few years, during the summer of my sophomore year at Trevecca Nazarene University, I had the privilege to serve as an intern at the Lamb's Club. B.J. and Sheila were in the early years of their marriage and living at the Lamb's. I didn't know Sheila much at that time, but thought, what kind of woman could marry B.J.? It turns out a pretty special one. At the time, I was not looking to be anyone's protégé, but little did I know I was being groomed to be an intern and B.J. was becoming my mentor. I learned many life lessons that summer that have served me well.

There is one particular incident that stands out as a seminal moment in my spiritual development. The Lamb's Mission, or "Club" as it was called, was located on West 44th street, just off Times Square in the Broadway theater district. In fact, the Lamb's doubled as a theater and a church. It also housed a soup kitchen in the basement, amongst many other ministries. All this happened right in the heart of the most influential city in the world. On some weekends, one of the rooms on the first floor was converted into a coffee house. It's the same room where B.J. first "called me out" as a teenager. About the time the theaters were emptying out, members of the church would mull around Times Square and pass out these clever pamphlets (we called them tracts) that capitalized on the themes of the current Broadway shows. The tracts weaved the Gospel story into the plot lines of the shows. People would then be invited back to the Lamb's for free coffee, snacks, and conversation. The church members practiced hospitality and steered interactions to personal testimony and Gospel conversation. I was assigned to the front door as a sort of greeter/bouncer. I was instructed to be mindful of any homeless folks who might show up and seek entrance into the coffee house. I was OK with the greeter job description, but not sure how to screen for those who didn't meet the profile of the intended audience for this event. Then it happened. A man who obviously fit the profile of homeless presented at the door. As graciously as I knew how, I tried to explain to him how the night's event was focused as an outreach to the "theater" crowd. I extended an invitation to return in the morning for our breakfast for the homeless. The man went away into the night and my heart was crushed. I returned to my room that night and cried. I told one of the staff what had happened. It was the great Joe Colazzi, who later become the longstanding Director at the Kansas City Rescue Mission. I described the man to Joe. He knew the man, tracked him down, and tried to undo any harm I may have done.

After getting my heart broken, I went to my room and dove into the Scriptures and landed in James, chapter 2.

Favoritism Forbidden

"My brothers and sisters, believers in our glorious Lord Jesus Christ must not show favoritism. 2 Suppose a man comes into your meeting wearing a gold ring and fine clothes, and a poor man in filthy old clothes also comes in. 3 If you show special attention to the man wearing fine clothes and say, "Here's a good seat for you," but say to the poor man, "You stand there" or "Sit on the floor by my feet," 4 have you not discriminated among yourselves and become judges with evil thoughts?

Listen, my dear brothers and sisters: Has not God chosen those who are poor in the eyes of the world to be rich in faith and to inherit the kingdom he promised those who love him?"

I studied that scripture that night and demanded an audience with B.J. the next day. We went to the roof of the Lamb's and I gave him a sermon about how we should not show favoritism, and he graciously agreed. He said serving in the City is hard and if things were not right, why didn't I come back and do something about it? He went on to tell me that we did not need any more nice Christian boys; we had enough of those. We needed people who were radical in their walk. These were challenging words for a young man who had grown up in a relatively sheltered Christian home. The contrast of the truly blessed existence that I was so graciously afforded compared to that of a broken world, one that never had the privilege of such a godly home, was compelling. How could I continue to bask in the blessings that were mine, most of which were given to me and not of my own earning? We are blessed to be a blessing, not to build bigger barns for ourselves.

Well, that summer ended and I was forever changed. I approached graduation from college and had no real direction for my life, other than I wanted to help people. I had no prospects of how to make a living and support myself. It then occurred to me that B.J. was pretty connected and knew a lot of people, so I reached out to him to see if he had any leads for an unemployed college graduate. Two weeks later, he called me back with a proposition to come and serve the poor in NYC. I was excited by the offer and then he went on to ask if I would be willing to raise half my own support. Always a catch with B.J. I told him I would have to pray about it. A few months after graduation I was living in NYC, sleeping on a green crushed velvet couch in the newly organized New York Fellowship's office, located in the heart of the financial center of the world, just blocks from Wall Street. The next few years would set the compass for my life's work and mission.

I bounced around on couches for the next year, making lifelong friends who inspired me and graciously gave themselves to me.

They taught me how to share and showed me what Christian community looked like. Guys like Bob Muzikowski, Bill Lundeen, Father William Wilson, Brad Curl, and a host of other fascinating people who seemed to flow in and out of B.J.'s world. I got to rub shoulders with these good men and was the better for it. As a result, I learned that if I wanted to be great, I had to be around great people and one of the best things we can give away is our friends.

If working for B.J. and living in NYC wasn't enough of a culture shock, B.J. assigned me to work at St. George's Episcopal Church on the Lower East Side as a "street minister," whatever that was. The homeless lunch crowd soon elevated me by giving me the unearned title of Father Daryl. I was a fish out of water, trying to make sense of the liturgy with all the reading, sitting, standing, and kneeling. I eventually came to appreciate it and the realization that God's family had a much bigger tent than the box I had put Him in.

After about a year as an intern at the New York Fellowship, I announced to B.J. that I had decided to marry my college sweetheart. Like everyone else I told, I expected B.J. to be happy for me. Instead, he immediately challenged me and inquired as to whether this was the right one for me. I was a little put off by this and immediately went into defense mode (something B.J. can evoke in others) to explain our love for one another. Later, I came to appreciate that B.J. loved me enough to ask the tough questions when others hesitated to do so. He finally came around and even paid for our first night's stay of our honeymoon.

Upon the announcement of my nuptials, it became clear that couch surfing would not suffice for a young married couple, so B.J. arranged for me to move into one of the rectory apartments at St. George's Church. When I brought my bride to live with me there, we did not have a functioning kitchen and had to do our dishes in the tub. Eventually, we were able to remedy that inconvenience. After another year of service through the N.Y. Fellowship, I told B.J. that we had decided to move back to Tennessee and I was to become a youth pastor. He accused me of abandoning the city and selling out for a white picket fence in the suburbs. Maybe so, but the influences and impact of those experiences in the inner city have always left its imprint on me and still shape my life today. There are more stories that could be told but to just highlight a few of the ongoing effects of B.J.'s impact on my life: I have an adopted nephew as a result of B.J.'s friendship, and my nephew has a blessed and loving family. For the past 27 years, I have been the Founder and Executive Director of Welcome Home Ministries, a faith based non-profit in Nashville, TN that operates 8 homes and serves 68 men who are under our care and recovering from alcohol and drug addiction.

Thanks to my dear friend and mentor, B.J. Weber, for selflessly giving his life away for the sake of the Kingdom and the eternal ripple effects of his ministry.

Daryl Murray is the founder and executive
director of Welcome Home Ministries in
Nashville, TN, which provides safe, clean, healthy,
and sober living communities of compassionate
care for men who have been homeless, addicted,
or recently released from prison. Since 1992, the
ministry has grown to currently provide 68 beds
in a total of eight recovery homes.

Welcome to New York: One Crazy Place!

By Bob Saxon

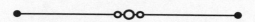

I have had the privilege of knowing B.J. for more than 40 years. I met B.J. in the late 1970s at First Presbyterian Church in Aurora, Illinois, where my family and I attended and B.J. served as a pastoral intern.

B.J. and I seemed to hit it off right away. We were both the same age and we shared many of the same interests, including our love of sports.

He was young and single and had rugged good looks, an engaging personality, and a great sense of humor. In getting to know B.J., it was evident he had deep spiritual roots, his life having been radically changed by a personal encounter with Jesus. His testimony was remarkable and compelling.

While serving at "First Pres," B.J. led a Bible study in which my wife, Joyce, and I took part. I have heard B.J. preach on several occasions and have participated in several men's retreats, which he has led. B.J. inspired and challenged me in my faith journey with not only his words but also his actions. I have drawn strength and encouragement from him.

Our family readily adopted B.J. We enjoyed many meals together at our home. Being single meant that cooking was not one of his favorite activities. Often B.J. would just show up on our doorstep, just in time for dinner. How convenient! He became a welcomed part of our family. Since I came from a family of three sisters and no brothers, B.J. became like the brother I never had. It was wonderful hanging out with him. Sometimes we would jog together. Other times we would just sit and talk. I loved the time we spent together. I have always felt a very special connection with B.J.

B.J. makes up nicknames, whether you want him to or not. Because of his warm and engaging personality, he fit in nicely with our family. I remember B.J. connecting with our son Brett (when he was age 8) and our daughter Brooke (then age 1). B.J. would bounce Brooke on his knee while holding her sucker as she licked it. He affectionately began referring to her as "Brooklyn." The name stuck and he still refers to her as "Brooklyn" to this day.

One of the things that stood out about B.J. was his commitment to following God's direction for his life, regardless of what that meant. But we knew God had special plans for him.

One day B.J. announced that he felt a calling to minister in New York City. New York is a fast-paced, intimidating place, especially if you are from the Midwest. It is not a place for the weak or timid. Well, B.J. being B.J., he hit the ground running. He started a street ministry where he served for five years in rescue and recovery efforts for addicts, prostitutes, teenage runaways, and the homeless while co-pastoring a mission church in Times Square. It was a work God had called him to and he pursued it with unbridled passion, a passion that has characterized his life. B.J. has always had a keen desire to serve those in need, especially the less fortunate and hurting. His experience at the mission would serve him well in the years ahead.

I have visited B.J. in New York several times over the years. On one occasion, I vividly remember coming with my family to see firsthand what B.J. was up to. Staying at the Lamb's Mission in the heart of New York and seeing B.J. in action was an eye opening and humbling experience I shall never forget.

In 1984, B.J. founded the New York Fellowship. As part of this very diverse ministry, he served as the chaplain for the New York Yankees for more than a dozen years. I remember meeting B.J. at the old, historic Yankee Stadium. The Yankees were playing the Detroit Tigers that day, and B.J. invited me to join him in the Yankee clubhouse before the game. He gave me a special badge and we marched right past all the security personnel directly into the Yankee clubhouse. Being a big baseball fan, I thought I had died and gone to heaven. What a historic place, a place once occupied by some of the greatest ball players of all time: Mickey Mantle, Yogi Berra, Whitey Ford, Roger Maris, etc. I felt like I was living in a dream world. We left the clubhouse and walked down the tunnel to the Yankee dugout, another sacred place. I sat on the bench and looked out over the field where so many historic games have taken place, thinking that I may be sitting in the exact same place as one or more of those legendary Yankees of the past. Wow! What a thrill of a lifetime!! I love telling this story and have told it many times. We left the clubhouse and B.J. asked me to follow him up to the upper deck where Yankee owner, George Steinbrenner, had his office. B.J. joined Mr. Steinbrenner and asked me to take a seat in the stands just below his office window. As soon as I sat down, an older gentleman approached and sat down next to me. We talked baseball for a while and then he finally excused himself and left. Shortly after he left, B.J. emerged and asked me if I knew who I was talking to. I had no idea. He said, "That was Hall of Fame Detroit Tiger broadcaster Ernie Harwell." I knew of Ernie Harwell but had no idea what he looked like. Having the opportunity to talk baseball with a legendary broadcaster like Ernie Harwell was a special treat and made the day complete.

On another occasion, B.J. and I were walking down the street one morning to a coffee shop. We approached an intersection and saw a lady in a late model sedan pull over to the curb. She threw open her door without looking only to have the door sheared off by a cab speeding through the instruction. The cabbie slams on his breaks, gets out of his cab and approaches the lady who immediately begins pummeling him with her fists. The cabbie did his best to defend himself, but it was not going well. A shouting match ensued. Things got ugly. We elected not to stay for the aftermath. Welcome to New York. One crazy place!

B.J. has an uncanny ability to relate to a variety of people in all stations of life, whether it be a drug addict, prostitute, or Wall Street executive. Over the years he has made himself available to countless numbers of people who were in need or hurting. The diversity of his ministry exemplifies this spirit.

Some friendships were meant to last a lifetime. That's how it has been with me and B.J. We may go long periods without seeing one another but when we do come together, it is like we have never been apart. The spark of friendship is instantly rekindled. That is a rare and special type of friendship for which I am so grateful. My wife and I have had the privilege of helping provide ongoing financial support to B.J. and the New York Fellowship for many years. It has been a joy to do so. I have shared with B.J. several times that my wife and I are intent on providing financial support to Christian ministries that have a real and lasting impact. "Bang for the buck," we call it. B.J. and the New York Fellowship are definitely "impact players" who provide lots of "spiritual bang for the buck." Countless lives have been touched and changed through this ministry.

Forty years of ministry in New York City is a noteworthy achievement. Congratulations! I don't know of another person who could have pulled this off as well as B.J. Weber. New York was tailor-made for him. Well done, good and faithful servant! There is more to come.

Bob Saxon was owner of the Tillers Nursing Home in Oswego, IL for 43 years, and is now happily retired.

Lost in a Faraway Place...

By Dan Fox

On a late summer Friday evening in 1980, I left my apartment near Times Square intending to just get a bite to eat—a sandwich, or a slice. I had no idea that little outing would completely change the trajectory of my life, or that it would lead me to my first encounter with B.J. Weber.

I moved to New York after college, like many of my friends, to pursue an acting career. I was definitely not pursuing God, but I know now that He was tirelessly pursuing me. When I rounded the corner on 47th and Broadway that night, I found a Christian rock band playing right there in Duffy Square, amid the cabs whizzing by, the horns honking, and the neon signs flashing. This was not an everyday event in my neighborhood, so I stopped to listen. When the band took a break, a young man took the microphone and started talking about Jesus. He presented the Gospel in an honest, clear, compelling way, without any condemnation, and with real compassion. As he finished his talk, he invited anyone who wanted to know more about this life of faith to come to a gathering that

Sunday evening at the nearby Lamb's Manhattan Church of the Nazarene.

After buying something for dinner I walked back to my apartment, surprised that I could not get the words of the street preacher out of my mind. For several months or longer I had been feeling more and more empty, less and less satisfied with my whole acting career, and deeply unhappy with the life I was living. I had been selfish and dishonest and manipulative in too many relationships, and had hurt too many people. The "aw shucks," nice Midwestern guy image I presented to the world had become a useful tool to earn people's trust, a trust which I too often abused. I was sick of who I had become and needed to talk to somebody about it. Like the prodigal son in the Gospel parable, I was finally "coming to myself." I was living under the weight of shame and self-hatred, and I knew only God could deal with that.

As the man with the microphone had suggested, I made my way to the Lamb's that Sunday night. It is amazing to me, still, that it was only three blocks from my apartment. I remember walking into a candlelit room with a huge fireplace on the first floor. There was a crowd of people there, but the first person to greet me was a guy a few years older than I was who looked more like a football player or a bar bouncer than a pastor. He introduced himself as B.J. and said he was on staff at the church, and he wanted to know about me. He asked, "What are you all about?" We sat down and I told him who I was and that I was an actor. Then I quickly found myself pouring out my confession about the life I was living and how sorry I was and how I hated myself for the things I had done. As I talked and cried, I watched his expression for some trace of shock (this guy was a pastor) at my story. There was none. More than anything I sensed that B.J. had felt exactly what I was feeling and was sharing the pain with me. He called me "brother," and talked to me for a long time about the mercy and love of Jesus. From B.J. there was no pronouncement of judgment on my past. I knew I had been wandering, lost in a far country, far from God and living a joyless, empty life. He shared enough of his own story to let me know that he, too, had once been estranged from God and had been just as desperate. He offered the assurance of pardon and welcomed me into a new life in Christ.

At the Lamb's I found an amazing group of new friends. There were so many who showed me kindness and helped me begin to live as a follower of Jesus. There were actors and writers and producers and all sorts of brilliant, gifted people who had chosen to live in intentional community with other Christians. They answered my questions, encouraged me, shared their own faith stories, and showed me the love of God. It was a sweet time. B.J. invited me to join him and a few other guys my age one morning a week to study the Bible together, to support and encourage one another, and to be accountable to one another. The concept of Christian friendship was new to me, and that group showed me what real friendship could be. We met faithfully for several months and then agreed to meet twice a week. B.J. poured himself, week after week, into me and those other young men. He talked to us like he was just another guy. He was brutally honest about his own struggles and temptations, and that gave us permission to be open and transparent, too.

Since my apartment was only a couple of blocks from the Lamb's, I hung out there a lot in those next few months. I had been a singer and played the guitar and piano, so I got involved in the music ministry and was invited to assist with leading the singing for some of the services. I had no idea then, doing this for the first time, that I would go on to become a worship leader and that I would lead worship in the church for over thirty years. It has been one of the great joys of my life. For so long, as an actor, I had considered any gifts and talents I had to be mine. They belonged to me. Now I began to understand that all we have, all we are, including our gifts and talents, belongs to God and gifts are given to us so that we might glorify Him and bless other people.

B.J. introduced me to the faith and Christian community at the Lamb's and discipled me as a young believer. He helped me to see that a life of faith and choosing to follow Jesus could be an adventure. He was fearless and showed me that being a Christian is not supposed to be a safe, comfortable little life. He took risks, and sometimes had disappointments and failures, yet he taught me not to live in or be defined by my own failures. The Christian life he modeled (and still does) at times could be scary, it could be costly, it could be painful, but it would never be boring.

Jesus does not invite us into a joyless life of pinched piety, solemn duty, and moral perfection. He calls us to an abundant life of shared laughter, joy, and celebration as well as shared sorrow, failure, and loss—and friendship. Jesus shared life with a group of friends and B.J. was (and is) all about friendship. He talked a lot about "just showing up," being available for others, especially when it is inconvenient. It is the fullest kind of life a person can experience, and B.J. has lived that life to the full. He has shown all of us how to live it. In looking back over the past forty years of my own life, I only wish I had followed his example more closely and risked more, given more of myself for Jesus and for others.

In late 1984, when the Lord had led us all to St. George's Episcopal Church, B.J. and Sheila had an important part in connecting me with the young woman who would become my wife. After I let them know I was very interested in a recent visitor to the church I had met and chatted with briefly, they strategically paired me up with her to help prepare part of a Sunday brunch after church at their apartment so we could get better acquainted. A few weeks later they invited us both to a dinner at an Italian restaurant in their neighborhood and not-so-randomly seated us next to each other. They were clever and willing co-conspirators, used by God in helping me to woo and win Kimberly Atherton's affection.

It was a joy, a little over a year later, to have B.J. officiate and be part of the celebration at our wedding. Our families have remained connected over the years, and I have been honored to provide music at the weddings of both Rachel and Max. I have been honored, too, to lead Christmas carols at the annual Weber Christmas party for many years, and to be part of the musical festivities at major birthday milestones for B.J.

When our son Brendan was in middle school, we could not afford to send him to Deerfoot Lodge, a well-known Christian summer camp for boys in upstate New York. B.J. made it possible for Brendan to go, for several years. The boundless generosity that for so long has been extended to me and Kimberly has also been shown to our son, all with the hope of drawing one more young man into a relationship with Jesus.

Almost forty years ago, my life was forever changed when I became a follower of Jesus. The person God used, more than any other, to introduce me to Jesus and to help me grow and mature in my new faith was B.J. Weber. The person who has shared, more than any other, his time and his heart and his life with me to show me what friendship in Christ looks like is B.J. He is the person who has demonstrated, more than anyone else I have ever met, how a life completely surrendered to God can bless countless others and literally change the world. He changed my world, and I will be forever grateful.

Happy 40th anniversary, brother.

Dan Fox is an actor, vocalist, pianist, guitarist, published songwriter, and music teacher. For more than 20 years he has served as a worship leader for three different churches in Connecticut, and as guest worship leader for other churches, conferences, and events.

Students Cheer:
"No B.J., No Hope!"

By Bob Muzikowski

In June 2019, my wife and I attended Opening Day for the Near West Little League on Chicago's west side. It was the 28th season of baseball and mentoring for Chicago's largest urban little league with thousands of inner-city youth being served, since we founded the organization when our own children were young. The League has always been less about baseball and more about mentoring, racial reconciliation, and Bible-based living in a fun way. We did not become Christians to be miserable! Today, many of the coaches, including my son, Bo Muzikowski (age 27), are former players. So the league has passed to another generation.

A week earlier, Chicago Hope Academy held commencement exercises as the Academy wrapped up its 14th academic year since we founded the school in 2005. Many of the students at Chicago Hope, the city's only non-denominational Christian High School, also played baseball in the League. Graduates of Hope Academy have gone on to the U.S. Naval Academy, the U.S. Air Force

Academy, Columbia University, Brown, Princeton, Northwestern, and Wheaton College, with many graduates entering the military.

None of this would have happened if not for a providential meeting on the Rugby Field in New York City in 1981. It was a fall Saturday afternoon and the nationally renowned Old Blue Rugby Club, of which I was starting forward, was hosting Old Green (Dartmouth alumni) at Randall's Island.

Old Blue won the first match, and I had begun the sideline party with a creative way of snorting cocaine in broad daylight. I had ground up an ounce, put it into a bright orange sippy cup, put on the cap, and inserted a straw. Who would think?

Meanwhile, young Reverend B.J. Weber was being tossed out of the second match for fighting. This is not an easy thing to do in rugby. "That guy is a priest! WTF!" exclaimed one of their teammates. Of course, I offered B.J. to snort from the cup.

Rev. B.J. declined but did pop open a beer. He invited me to his church, the Lamb's on 130 West 44th Street. I took it as a dare. I showed up the next morning, working on quite the hangover. Thus began the story of our intense 38-year friendship.

It took more than two years of B.J.'s persistent kindness and initiative, but after bailing me out of jail after a Maryland bar fight that took place on the eve of the Presidential Prayer Breakfast, B.J.

and Brad Curl led me to the Lord. Later that night back at home in New York City, I walked into my first AA meeting, and have been clean and sober ever since.

Around 18 months later, B.J. and Sheila held a barbecue at their home on East 32nd Street in Manhattan. One of Sheila's friends was JP Morgan trader Tina Wells. I was invited as B.J.'s friend and brought along a new friend I was supporting, a blind marathon runner named Tom O'Connor. I was helping him train for the NYC marathon, which we completed together in a very laudable 3:18. Of course, Tommy took an unabashed interest in Tina. "You sound very nice," he said. "Have you ever been on a blind date?" As providence would have it, Tina chose me instead of Tom.

Two years later B.J. presided over Tina's and my wedding in Nashville. The Old Blue Rugby Club played the Tennessee All Stars at noon in Nashville, so we scheduled the wedding at 6 p.m. My best man toasted through his broken ribs, and I sported a black eye. Tina handled us rowdy men with aplomb.

Six months later, Tina and I moved to Chicago and "by mistake" moved one block away from the Cabrini Green Housing project. It was there that we began our family of 7 children and became legal guardians for 4 others. It was there in 1991 that we started the largest inner-city Little League in the U.S. Later in 1995, B.J. and I also started the first Little League that NYC's Harlem had in 25 years; four hundred kids signed up the first day.

Throughout this time B.J. and I stayed in close touch. A month did not pass when we did not pray together, meet in person, or commiserate on the phone.

It is fair to say that if not for B.J.'s patience and counseling, there would be no Little Leagues, no Chicago Hope Academy, no Muzikowski family, and no thousand-fold harvest of souls.

Bob Muzikowski (Columbia University, B.A, M.B.A.) has built a thriving Northwestern Insurance business, while being co-founder, with his wife Tina, of the Chicago Hope Academy, with its award-winning sports teams, and the Chicago Near West Little League. He and Tina are parents to 7 children, all of whom attended Chicago Hope and (those old enough) went on to prestigious universities. A major motion picture, "Hardball," starring Keanu Reeves, was based on Bob's life, but left out the important element of his personal faith, which motivated Bob to write his own autobiography: *Safe at Home: The true and inspiring story of Chicago's Field of Dreams.*

THE TIME SQUARE MISSION YEARS: A PHOTO ALBUM

In Times Square. This album is credited to a 1979 Dubuque Telegraph Herald series and photographer © Paul Dagys

Praying for those in need.

Witnessing to hope in a dark place.

Befriending unusual characters.

Helping the addicted.

In front of the Lamb's Mission.

Rescuing the fallen.

B.J. and Sheila, newly engaged in 1979 on a NYC subway.

A day that changed our lives forever. August 2, 1980. (Photo courtesy of the Weber family)

The New York Fellowship

1985 to present

First Boots on the Ground

By Pam and Barry Abell

In the early dusk of evening, 35 years ago, we stood at a bus stop in front of the Friar Tuck restaurant in Montclair, NJ. We were waiting for a bus to arrive from NYC that carried B.J. and Sheila Weber, whom we had never met. We—Barry, a young municipal bond trader on Wall Street, and Pam, a mother and Bible study leader—had a deep desire to begin a personal ministry to the business community in NYC. We had witnessed too much greed, infidelity, and misplaced priorities. Longing to reach out with the Gospel and to offer a spiritual haven for seeking or lost souls, we had been directed to B.J. through a trusted national leader.

When the bus arrived and the doors opened, an attractive, poised Sheila stepped down first, followed by B.J. Instead of the sophisticated man in a pinstripe suit who we expected, B.J. emerged in western attire, including the boots and hat. Unabashed and friendly, he clasped our hands warmly with a broad smile. That memorable evening as we shared our first meal together became the foundation of the New York Fellowship! It was also the beginning of a deep, rich friendship that has spanned many seasons of life and ministry. God took four unlikely people, combining their common visions and prayers for the City, and built a Christ-centered ministry extending far beyond the borders of NYC.

We smile as we recall those early years of establishing the NYF. We "stumbled" prayerfully through creating a board of directors, locating a well-situated office, and financing staff and outreaches. The Lord was so faithful through this process and our inexperience. As B.J.'s personality and gifts emerged, it influenced the direction and tone of the ministry. We realized that we could not "put God in a box," nor B.J. for that matter! The NYF took on a more personal, intimate quality as B.J. came alongside individuals with a wide variety of needs. In a busy, fast-paced city, could there actually be a person who would care enough to help another in need? Yes, that person was B.J.! Soon his office and home were full of individuals being discipled, lives being transformed by love in human flesh and the Gospel. Many of these lives whom B.J. impacted went on to create other ministries, offshoots of the NYF. Just to name a few there was The Harlem Little League, an orphanage in Bolivia, the New Canaan Society, sport chaplaincies, countless ministers, and outreach to UN ambassadors. It was like God was saying to us, "I know you had NYC in mind, but I had a much bigger picture!" Basically, we just hung onto God and B.J.'s coattails and sailed along in directions we had never imagined.

Another offshoot ministry of the NYF was the establishment of a pregnancy crisis office directed by the dedicated Gloria Rhule. Through her counsel and help, many unborn babies were saved from abortion and placed into loving, adopted homes. The first little life, Jamie, is especially dear to our hearts. We followed his life for a few years and even had the blessing of tossing a football with him at our home at age six. That was a life-changing moment for Barry, in particular, fueling a passion to protect the unborn. That passion continues.

As our lives became more deeply intertwined with B.J. and Sheila's, God developed in us a desire to leave the workplace and go into full-time ministry as well. We followed that call in September 1990, becoming involved in marriage and family ministry. Through the last 35 years, the NYF and B.J. and Sheila have been so dear and special to us. The impact they have had on our lives is immeasurable! Our friendship is still deep despite time and distance, and God has shown us some incredible truths through them.

Here are just a few that have stayed with us over the years. First, never limit the Lord! Be open to His Spirit and be willing to follow in faith where He leads, even if it looks like a mountain. Secondly, place the needs of people before your own, remaining flexible and available. Have the heart of a servant. And third, expect the Lord to accomplish what may seem impossible! Pray and trust Him in all things.

B.J. and Sheila's energy and devotion to others is extraordinary.
Tears of compassion are a quality that defines B.J. and a quality
that the Lord has used mightily in guiding the direction of the
NYF. The Webers love all people, regardless of their station in life.
Sheila has been the voice of reason and organizational backbone
for B.J., who could, and often would, overextend himself in serving
others; but together they have created a comfortable, gracious
environment for all those fortunate to cross their paths, from the
very poor to the very wealthy. Yet, their tears of compassion are
equaled by their ability to see humor in the commonplace, and
not to take themselves too seriously. We love their ability to laugh
heartily, finding great joy in their friendships, family, and the Lord.
It has been one of the greatest and deepest blessings of our lives to
be called their friends and to play a small part in what God had in
mind 40 years ago!

*"Now to Him who is able to do exceedingly abundantly above all that we
ask or think, according to the power that works in us, to Him be glory in
the church by Christ Jesus to all generations, forever and ever. Amen."*
Ephesians 3:20-21

Barry and Pam Abell were the first board members of the New York Fellowship, and now serve as directors of Executive Ministries New Jersey. Barry received his Bachelor of Arts degree and worked as a municipal bond trader for 21 years on Wall Street. Pam received her Master of Science in elementary education. They lead Bible studies, retreats, and mentoring weekends for engaged and married couples.

An Unexpected Calling: Unplanned Babies

By Gloria Rhule

I t was not something on my five- or ten-year list of goals. I had never planned to work with women who found themselves in crisis due to an unplanned pregnancy. I had certainly been exposed to the conflicting views of the pro-life and pro-choice movements. In the 80s, the debate reached a fever pitch. A friend once remarked that Christians needed to DO something to help women rather than merely argue and demonstrate for their own position. I remember reflecting on this statement, but no action on my part came from it. Then the opportunity to "do something" came in the most unexpected way.

It was during this time of heated, and sometimes vitriolic, debates that B.J. and I were confronted with the needs of a young woman who had shockingly chosen to keep her unplanned pregnancy a secret. Following the child's birth, she realized she was ill-prepared to care for him. Suddenly it was no longer an issue of ideology or politics. It was about a mother's loving but heart-wrenching decision to make an adoption plan for her child; and B.J. and I along with others supported her during and after this process. As a result, the child became part of a family whom B.J. knew well, a family who also loved the infant and could care for and nurture him.

This event, though extremely unsettling, was the beginning of the New York Fellowship's Pregnancy Service, a ministry to assist women with unplanned pregnancies. To my surprise, B.J. invited me to direct it. To be honest, I was hesitant. I wasn't certain that I had the skill set that was required. However, B.J. encouraged me to believe that if I was willing and available, God would equip and use me. I accepted that invitation. Over the next few years, we at the New York Fellowship were intentional in helping women make a plan for the children they carried. For some it meant facilitating adoptions. For others it meant providing emotional and spiritual care as well as helping them secure the services they would need to parent the children themselves.

The New York Fellowship's Pregnancy Service was not something that was part of B.J.'s five- or ten-year ministry plan either. As was his practice though, he saw the need, responded to it, and remained open to how God's plan might involve him in doing further work in that area. When you listen for and serve an infinite God, the probability that He will use you to accomplish more than you planned is great. B.J. was His servant. B.J. was listening.

Gloria Rhule was director of the N.Y. Fellowship's Women's Ministry and Pregnancy Service from 1986 to 1991. She later served as clinical supervisor and project director on multiple research trials in the Department of Psychology at Penn State University.

The Orphans of Bolivia

By Anne Grizzle

B.J.'s work with the poor in New York City was a source of inspiration for his own mentor, Father William Wilson. While Fr. William was still living in the monastery, he visited B.J. in Times Square. After seeing the sort of dire poverty and pain that was all around, Fr. William was led to leave his cloistered monastery home in order to live among the poor. Bolivia is home to many of the poorest of the poor in our hemisphere, so Fr. William ended up in the Quechua village of Aramasi, high in the Andes, among people who were destitute, without clean water, electricity, or health care.

Although he came to simply live among them, pray, and continue his life as a monk, mothers would come to him with dying babies and villagers with severe health needs. The book he had on hand, *When There is No Doctor*, did not seem adequate. So he called his friend B.J. to see if he could help fund a simple clinic for the poor in Aramasi. B.J. called his friends in New York working on Wall

Street, and friends from around the country, to ask them to make this dream a reality.

Without B.J.'s friendship with Father William—and then with so many Christians in America—these hearts and bodies would yet still be breaking. Instead, the Mary Mahoney Clinic and the work of Amistad Mission began.

Later, the need for a respite space for workers led to the building of La Morada retreat house in Cochabamba. And when Fr. William was asked to be a patron of a nearby clinic, he stumbled across Solomon Klein Orphanage where the filth and horror left a "lump in his throat he hoped he would never forget." Dogs ran through the halls, and there were three to four babies in a crib, lying untended and catatonic.

Father William said, "God tricked me. I cannot walk away from what I have just seen." So this monk with a heart for the poor partnered with his disciple and friend B.J. Weber—who had friendships that could mobilize resources—and they took on two government orphanages (which had been run by thugs and a mafia-type ring) to care for these abandoned orphaned children. When the partnership with the government of Bolivia became untenable, they once again imagined and reached out to friends to build La Villa, a large acreage and beautiful multiple home facility, with a Mama and Tia for each house of 10 children.

William, the spiritual leader living on the ground in Bolivia, and B.J., the minister in New York City with friends around the U.S., partnered to create with God a mission of friendship across cultures and continents and classes. These two envisioned the creation of the Amistad Mission in Bolivia, but they also traveled all over the U.S. telling the story and speaking to anyone who would listen to gain friends for the poor. From their invitation, hundreds of church groups and Christ-seekers, young and old, have visited Amistad Mission and had their lives transformed in friendship with the poor in Bolivia.

Our own Amistad journey began with a call from B.J. to my husband, David, while they were in a Times Square men's Bible study. B.J. told David about his friend Father William and the need to pitch in some money to create a clinic. We supported that clinic and the work for quite a few years before giving in to B.J.'s insistence that we "come and see." Then the staff and children of Amistad became our friends and return trips upon trips were made. Amistad became a part of our family.

Editor's note: As Amistad Mission Board Chair for many years, Anne Grizzle helped transition the mission from its origins as a project of the New York Fellowship to become its own self-sustaining charity. Her personal influence in Bolivia still abounds—Anne's own sons established a Children's Olympics, her friends traveled for spiritual retreats and volunteerism, and the mission thrives today because her leadership turned a start-up project among friends into the well-run organization it is today.

Anne F. Grizzle is a licensed family therapist and ordained Episcopal priest. A graduate of Harvard University, with a Master of Social Work from Columbia University, she runs "Strength for the Journey" retreats at her home, The Bellfry at Broadview Ranch, near Lexington, VA. Also residents of Washington, D.C., she and her husband, David, co-chair World Vision's campaign to raise $1 billion to combat extreme poverty across the globe.

Reviving the Historic Bowery Mission

By Ed Morgan

I met B.J. Weber for the first time when I was the newly minted president of the Bowery Mission, driving my old Buick into New York from Chappaqua to try to save a 100-year-old ministry. From a couple of friends, I heard about this guy who ran something called the New York Fellowship. I couldn't exactly figure out what he did, but I knew he was highly respected in New York and he knew everybody, so I figured I needed to go see him.

I was invited over to his office in the Calvary-St. George's Parish house—a totally cool place overlooking Gramercy Park. I was amazed. "How did you get this office?" I asked. He never actually told me! I never thought that ten years later I would be on the vestry of the same Parish and we would be working together to bring renewal into this historic church.

The first day we just talked about ministry in New York. He did indeed know everyone, and it turned out that he had a rare combination of gifts. He had a heart for the poor and a heart for top executives in New York. What a combination. Of course, he saw right away that there was a significant chance to bring the Bowery Mission back to life and to see lives transformed by the Gospel.

I told him about the new contract we had with the City of New York to run one of their shelters down in Alphabet City on the Lower East Side. We agreed to talk more about that later.

In the meantime, we talked about a more pressing need of mine. The headquarters of Christian Herald Association was in Chappaqua, New York, but Christian Herald had always run NYC's Bowery Mission, and was closing its Christian Herald magazine. So, we wanted to focus solely on a Matthew 25 ministry to the poor and bring the organization back into the city. B.J. had some interesting thoughts about the Chappaqua property, of course—a place which was a former convent on 40 acres. He brought Jamie and Carolyn Copeland in to figure out how that property could be used for the Kingdom. This was the first time I saw B.J. the Visionary in action. As it turned out, we needed the money from the Chappaqua property to survive and ended up selling it to a developer to everyone's disappointment. But that was when I first saw what an important ally B.J. Weber could be if you were a friend.

However, I think the most influential thing that B.J. ever did for me was to exhort me like this: "Brother, you have to move into

New York City and be part of the ministry community here. You cannot expect God to bless the Bowery Mission unless you are right there understanding what it's like to be on the streets in New York. You need to give up your suburban life and become a New Yorker and let God bless your ministry." He would not let go of this point. He kept after me and so began our great adventure—17 years of being full-time residents in Manhattan. That would not have happened without my wonderful friend who dedicated his life to serving in the world's greatest city for 40 years himself. I believe his counsel was the key to the blessing that the Bowery Mission enjoyed under my leadership for nearly 20 years.

Then there was the whole Avenue D Men's Ministry story—the government-funded, faith-based opportunity we were given, maybe the first of its kind in the nation, and certainly the first in New York. I didn't know much about finding people who were good at doing personal life-transforming ministry to street people. All I knew was that I had a beautiful new building the City was giving us for free and a budget to go with it. One of B.J.'s cadre of young men was Bobby Polito, who understood the importance of ministering to the poor and its central part in the Gospel. Bobby had moved to NYC to be discipled by B.J. and was running a fitness center at the time, while looking for ministry opportunities.

B.J. nominated him to run the Avenue D Center, I hired him, and the rest is history. The Center became the highest performing shelter in the New York City Department of Homeless Services system. Ninety percent of the men who graduated clean and sober were still clean and sober a year later! It was amazing. Bobby designed a program which was truly holistic for New York men on the streets—a program no one had actually seen in New York before. B.J. mentored Bob and built an advisory board of business leaders from his extensive connections. I was amazed, and I was a hero. Later on, we took many of the same principles and incorporated them into the privately funded Bowery Mission Life-Transformation Recovery Program. In the hundreds of hours B.J. had spent with men on the streets and men from every walk of life, he learned how to make the Gospel come alive through genuine, unconditional caring. His experience translated into a program that built a wonderful opportunity for the Bowery Mission during that season.

Our friendship went on as our kids grew up and we both became mature leaders—at least on certain days!

Sidenote: Years later, Bob Polito went on to develop other faith-based, government-funded partnerships under Governor Tommy Thompson; then he later worked as an executive at HHS when Thompson became the U.S. Secretary for the Department of Health and Human Services. It was a long way from Polito's early years running an athletic center, and it all started when Polito met B.J. during his college days as a football player for Penn State. B.J. led the chapel service at the National Championship the year Penn State won, and he invited Bob to come to NYC to be mentored and grow in Christian discipleship. This led to Bob's job at the Bowery Mission Avenue D Center, which later opened doors that set his future in motion.

When another opportunity came up to work with B.J. on a very significant project for the Gospel in New York, I was all ears. The Parish of Calvary and St. George's is a church with a rich New York history—in fact, it was the historic church of J.P. Morgan. Rev. Tom Pike, the long-term rector, was a close friend of B.J. and Sheila. Tom had marched with Martin Luther King Jr. in the early days of the civil rights movement and was one of the longest serving Episcopal rectors in New York City. Through B.J.'s ministry in Tom's life, the church began to experience profound spiritual renewal. Through B.J.'s influence, a strategic group of evangelical friends, including my family, joined him at St. George's Church, a beautiful facility that later became the wedding site for my youngest son.

After Rev. Pike's retirement, I ended up on the Vestry and chairing the search committee to find the first evangelical rector for this historic Parish in many decades. What a great project and what a wonderful task force we formed to make this happen.

Through this project, my wife Judy and I learned the beauty of the liturgy and found a whole new richness in worship, which has influenced our lives ever since. We spent eight years in the Parish of Calvary and St George's. It was hard work and sometimes frustrating, but it was an experience we will never forget. It would not have happened without B.J.

As we move into our mature years together, I am tremendously grateful for B.J.'s influence in my life. The Lord has given him such a gift of personal discipleship and exhortation. May our friendship continue forever.

Ed Morgan is president emeritus of the Bowery Mission, and founder and principal of Inspirational Leadership, LLC, dedicated to the needs of non-profit CEOs and entrepreneurs. Ed is a creative and seasoned leader with uniquely broad qualifications developed over more than 40 years of successful Fortune 10 and nonprofit leadership experience. He and his wife Judy have three married sons and 10 grandchildren, and spend time in Manhattan, Connecticut, and Vero Beach, FL.

Paying the Love Forward:
Our Miracle Adoption

By George Lilja

You have many dreams and goals when you are young. Mine involved excelling in sports and someday starting a family. My wife Meg's dreams and goals were to excel at college, get a degree, then get married and start a family with children. Meg and I had always dreamed of holding a newborn baby in our arms and smelling the fresh new life and gift that God gives you when you have children.

All our dreams were coming true. First we were off to the University of Michigan, then we fell in love and enjoyed the beautiful fall Saturdays surrounded by 100,000 University of Michigan football fans, cheering on the Wolverines, where I played in the "Big House."

After graduation Meg was off to Rochester, Minnesota to work for IBM and I was off to Los Angeles to play in the National Football League for the Los Angeles Rams. One year after college, Meg and

I got married and began dreaming about starting a family (Psalm 127:4-5).

My NFL travels started when I was picked up by the New York Jets football team in the fall of 1983. Here is where B.J. and Sheila Weber came into our lives, and little would we know how much they would help write one of the best chapters of our lives.

B.J. Weber was asked to speak to the New York Jets football team in chapel service one Saturday evening at the hotel where the Jets stayed the night before our game. He spoke to the handful of Christian athletes who attended and invited me and my wife Meg along with some other teammates to his New York City home.

One of B.J.'s strengths that God gave him is being vulnerable for God and trusting in Him to connect with all kinds of people. B.J. has shared the love of Jesus with countless numbers of people, each of whom have a story to tell on how God used B.J. to change their lives.

This is our remarkable story. After we left New York City so I could play football in Cleveland for the Cleveland Browns, Meg and I had been married for five years and were still excited to start a family. With much prayer and anticipation, we waited for God to give us that first child. Meg grew up only having one brother, so she wanted to have many children so that our kids would have brothers and sisters to grow up with. I came from a family of eight kids, so I was looking forward to having a large, close family as well.

Sometimes our plans and timing are not God's plans and timing. As the years passed by, we began to realize we were going to have problems getting pregnant. Sometimes God is quietly working, and in the background He is preparing our hearts to reveal His plan for our good and His glory.

We spent many sleepless, and often tearful, nights wondering what God was doing by not allowing us to have children naturally. This is where God used B.J. to bring about His plans for our future family.

B.J. has the gift of faithfulness. He would call once in a while to say hello and remind us that he loved us. One day as Meg was opening a letter from the Cleveland Clinic containing more bad news and to notify her of a future (painful) procedure, the telephone rang. It was B.J. and he listened, prayed, and wept with Meg as she told him about our painful journey.

A few months later, B.J. let us know about a pregnant young woman, referred to him through her relatives. She had her own set of struggles and felt led toward adoption. B.J. said: "Let's pick a date next week, and Sheila and I will fast and pray with you to fully ask God for clarity and direction." It turned out, Meg's cycle swung around on the day of the fast, and we were back at the

Cleveland Clinic for another infertility procedure.

We told the doctor we had an opportunity to adopt and asked his opinion. He said, "If I were you two, I would seriously consider adopting this child, because you both are going to have a hard time having biological children." My jaw just about hit the floor and my heart sank when I heard what the doctor had to say about our situation.

At least we had our answer from God, so we began to dream about adopting. It was hard not to guard our hearts after so much disappointment, but we were already smitten by the little baby we hadn't met yet. Our labor pains were navigating the interstate legal hurdles. But on a lighter note, believe it or not we got a call from our VISA card company to inform us of suspicious, sudden activity at the Babies-R-Us store. Meg joyfully told him about our upcoming adoption.

B.J. flew to Cleveland after our daughter arrived. The Cleveland Browns head coach, Marty Schottenheimer, gave me a day off from 2-a-day training camp practices to pick up our newly adopted baby. B.J. spent all morning with the precious birthmother, being there for her through her grief and loss, and then he was at the courthouse that afternoon with Meg and me as we navigated the legal paperwork.

At 5:00 p.m. that day, we were finally allowed to meet our new baby girl in the hospital nursery. Our years of tears and sorrow turned to tears of joy. Our Danielle was the most beautiful baby ever born on this earth. God used B.J. to bring us this beautiful baby to fill our aching and longing arms and to answer the prayers that we had prayed for many years.

I have always wondered in amazement what it was about B.J. that gave him his drive and passion to grow God's Kingdom, a quality I so greatly admire about him. I think I found my answer in one of the disciples by the name of Peter, who reminded me most of B.J., always jumping out of the boat to experience God and His love (Matthew 14: 22-33). One of the more memorable conversations Jesus had with Peter was after His resurrection and He found Peter on the shores of the Sea of Galilee returning to his fishing life (John 21:15-17). Three times, Jesus asked Peter if he loved Him. Peter said yes and Jesus replied to him "feed my sheep." Finally, the third time Jesus asked Peter if he loved Him, Peter answered, "You know I love you Lord, you know all things." Then Jesus said, "Feed my sheep."

Like the disciple Peter, B.J. is so grateful for what the Lord has done for him and the beautiful family God has given him, that B.J. has committed his life to "feeding God's sheep." Meg, my adoptive daughter Danielle, and I have been on the receiving end of God's love for us through everything B.J. did by helping us adopt this beautiful baby girl that has grown up to be a wonderful Christian woman, now married herself and praying to start her own family today.

For years, every time Meg and I retold our adoption story, we would be brought to tears of joy realizing what a dear Christian brother and friend we had in B.J., who put himself out there sacrificially for us, so that Meg and I could experience the joy of starting a family of our own.

I have always admired and been inspired by B.J.'s willingness to be used by God, no matter what the circumstances, to grow God's Kingdom. He would be talking to a homeless person on the streets of New York City one minute, and then sharing God's love the next minute to a millionaire on Wall Street, pointing both of them to the love of Jesus Christ.

Many times I look at our beautiful daughter, Danielle, and it reminds me of the time in my life where B.J. was used by God to bring a child to a Christian couple who prayed for a long time to fill their longing arms with a child that they could love and raise to experience God's love. My wife and I are also amazed how God used this awesome woman (Danielle's birth mother) to give us this precious gift of a child who is growing into the beautiful woman that she is today.

Meg and I are forever grateful that God brought B.J. into our lives and we are trying to "pay the love forward to others," as an example of how B.J. lives his everyday life.

Editor's Note: After age 18, Danielle joyfully reconnected with her birth mother, who had remarried and had another child, Danielle's half-sister. Many years later, Danielle reconnected with her birth father and maintains a loving relationship with all her family members. Both Meg and George, along with Danielle's birth mother, sweetly celebrated Danielle's recent wedding together.

George Lilja is currently a businessman in the Midwest, and was an offensive lineman in the National Football League for the Los Angeles Rams, New York Jets, Cleveland Browns, and Dallas Cowboys. He played college football at the University of Michigan.

The Godson

By Benjamin Grizzle

"I have been called by God to New York City, and I will die here."
Spoken to—really, over—17-year-old me hours after I arrived in
Manhattan for my first summer internship at Goldman Sachs, B.J.'s
laconic, unqualified embrace of his calling will reecho in my heart
to the end of my days.

B.J. Weber is my godfather. Though reflecting no merit of mine,
the title might as well be on my resume for how often I brandish it
with pride. He has set the standard for this role unattainably high.
My life and that of my family bear the indelible marks of his care
over a lifetime.

My parents, contemporaries of the Beejmeister, came to New York
themselves from poor Southern families after graduate school.
Dad was a Wall Street lawyer; Mom was a social worker in Spanish
Harlem. Relatively new to charismatic faith through InterVarsity
at Harvard and having grown up in the tepid waters of Southern
cultural Christianity, my parents were encouraged and inspired by

B.J.'s passion for Jesus and the poor. His discipleship, by teaching and example, cultivated a missional lifestyle and generosity commitments that my family carries to this day and now into my generation.

When I was a kid, conservative Christianity had many evangelical parents fleeing cities for homogenous suburban bubbles, where their kids wouldn't run into any of the troubling, unseemly contemporary analogs of Jesus's women of ill-repute and tax collectors: drug users/dealers, the sexually promiscuous, gay people, greedy Wall Street types. But B.J.—like his son Max (an NYC firefighter) now does with literal fires—runs toward cultural conflagrations and personal crises rather than cowering in faithless fear. Commutes from the suburbs are the death of relationships on both ends. Cities are reliably on the leading and redemptive edge of culture. Proximity breeds intimacy, and nowhere is that truer than in New York, the greatest city on planet Earth. Beej loves Jesus, but he's quite an evangelist for the Big Apple and cities generally. He was a champion of New York since well before groups such as City to City and books like *To Change The World* made urban ministry the hip, strategic place to be for young evangelicals.

When I was an unreasonable middle schooler, B.J. wrote back with sympathetic but godly counsel to my angry letters about my parents' many shortcomings. He gave me my first hunting knife, which I have used for the last 20 years, and will doubtless pass on to my own kids. And then when I got the opportunity to come to

New York for an internship the summer after I graduated from high school, B.J. and Sheila generously offered me the ground floor of their brownstone.

When I got to 232 East 32nd Street that June of 1999, B.J. immediately took this Texas kid to his local Mexican place, in hindsight probably not to make me feel at home, but rather to show me NYC's got it as good as Texas. He ordered four of "your coldest beers" knowing full well I wasn't that far from starting to shave, and then told me his life's story and journey to Jesus in New York. That story concluded with his little-veiled critique of how modern-day missionaries go do their stints abroad, but generally eventually come back to wherever comfortable place whence they came. In contrast, missionaries from earlier eras, B.J. explained, moved to a place, married locals, gave their children local names that would sound weird if they ever went "home," gave those children in marriage to local spouses, and then they died and were buried there, not even in death returning to their homeland. Just like our Lord Jesus, they gave up their comfort and inherited identity, went where they were called, and poured themselves out unto death. And that's when those words fell: "I have been called by God to New York City, and I will die here."

I remember as a young man watching Matthew Broderick as Colonel Robert Gould Shaw in *Glory*, shot down on the sandy battlements of Fort Wagner, SC, his body becoming a stepping stone for the next nameless soldier who himself was shot down, and provided a firm step for the next man. Shaw gave his dignity and title to lead one of the Union's first all-black regiments in the Civil War, and ultimately gave his life in pursuit of that tactical objective that was never captured. Ever after I have thought, "I want to live my life for a cause so great that my life would be worth it if all I serve is as a stepping stone for the man coming after me in pursuit of that ultimate objective." B.J. is such a man who sees so clearly the Jesus who called him to this City and this work, and is running hard after Him with all that is within him, and will surely stumble bloodied into the arms of his Savior at the finish line having left his all on the field.

My lifetime's memories of B.J. are punctuated by great meals, generous hospitality, earthy jokes, unself-conscious probing of the depths of strangers and life-long friends alike, and spontaneous reflective overflows from the deep wells of his interior life. B.J. cries more than any man I know—for joy at my wedding and meeting my kids, in grief when he was the first person I called when my brother-in-law was killed, in ecstatic reflection on his Blessed Lord Jesus on any old Wednesday night in a room of mostly strangers, now new friends. But he is also in most respects the best template I have of manly virtues: physical courage, social confidence, practical competence, insatiable intellectual curiosity, life of the party, boundlessly generous, fiercely romantic lover of his bride and adorer of his children, leader of men, deft but forceful wielder of his considerable authority. More than any man but my own father, B.J. Weber has exemplified what a real man of

God is: one with a tender heart, but hard feet from getting after the hard work of life.

B.J., I love you, and could not be prouder to call you my godfather. I feel keenly—though with great gratitude—the burden of the legacy you have entrusted to me by your prodigal investment. May the stories in this book—a small remnant of the countless others that will only be retold generations hence—be a small down payment on the celebration of gratitude that surely awaits you, good and faithful servant.

Benjamin Grizzle, a magna cum laude graduate of Harvard University, is a Managing Director at Goldman, Sachs, & Co. He and his wife Heather have four children and are part of the Leadership Council of Church of the City New York.

The Man Who Makes You Laugh

By Bill Snyder

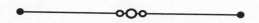

I first met B.J. in 1984 at a luncheon event in New York City. Soon after, Dave Balch invited me to attend the Beaver Street Bible Study that B.J. lead. What first impressed me about B.J. was that this man of deep Christian faith, hard-earned wisdom, and directness was also a great, fun-loving guy who loved people and enjoyed life to the fullest. That's a rare combination. I've marveled at it often in others, but never like what I saw in B.J.

Over the years, I would encourage B.J. to visit Israel. Borrowing from an Israeli archaeologist friend of mine, I'd say, "Beej, you have to go to Israel. Now you read the Bible in black and white. After you've been to Israel, you'll read it in living color!"

Then it happened. B.J. was going on a pilgrimage to Israel. What a coincidence, I was going to Israel around the same time but on a different trip. We compared schedules. "When are you going to be there, Beej?" It was the same week I would be there. "Let me see your itinerary," I asked. We would be in Tiberias on the Sea of

Galilee on the same 2 days. "Where are you staying?" B.J. couldn't recall so I gave him my hotel address and asked him to leave his local address at the front desk. When I arrived at my hotel, I had a message waiting. You guessed it—Beej was staying at the same hotel.

We got together over dinner that night with Sheila, Barry and Pam Abell, and my Israeli archaeologist friend Micha Ashkenazi, who was a member of the team that discovered the Pontius Pilate Stone during the excavation of Caesarea in 1961. (The stone was hugely significant for validating the time, history, and events of Christ's life.) During our conversation, I mentioned that I had stayed at this hotel three times before and my favorite thing to do was to get up before dawn, sit on a small jetty that pokes out into the Sea of Galilee, and watch the sun come up over the Golan Heights—a scene that is virtually unchanged from Jesus's time. Against the dawn sky you can still watch the black silhouettes of fisherman tending their nets as they glide past in their small boats.

About 5 a.m. the following morning, I grabbed my Bible and went out to the jetty, found a nearby folding chair, and took my position before the sunrise. It was dark and I was deep in thought. As the sun crept over the Golan Heights, I imagined, *This could be 2,000 years ago and it wouldn't look any different!* I opened my Bible and thanked God for letting me see such a wonderful sight. And then my meditation was shattered. **"IT IS I, BILL,"** a deep voice thundered just inches behind my head. Was this a locution from God? A Moses moment? I jumped right out of my seat—not figuratively, but literally—spinning around to see B.J. Weber roaring with laughter, his face lit up by the sunrise. I can still see the image of his face today like a photograph. Once I caught my breath, we were laughing like two little kids.

I imagine Jesus had a good laugh, too.

Bill Snyder is a Partner and Vice President of Charley, Inc., a New York City marketing and advertising firm specializing in brand development.

Tell It to Me Straight

By Bill Lundeen

During my last year of law school in Charlottesville, I accepted a position for the fall of 1984 as an associate attorney with a major firm in New York City. Little did I know the Lord would use the proximity of my office to draw me into remarkable relationships as B.J.'s ministry, the New York Fellowship, in those days was located only one block away.

I had a group of friends in the Washington, D.C. area, who I called to ask, "Who do you know in NYC?" One friend referred me to a men's Scripture study at the office of bond trader Barry Abell, whom my friend explained was the son-in-law of a key business leader in the D.C. group of friends.

What an extraordinary time. Barry explained that he and his wife Pam had made a formal presentation to a private family foundation for a grant to start a "fellowship" ministry in New York City. Everyone was thrilled for sufficient funds to pay one year's rent on a sizable and comfortable office above Dominic's Steak

House at 56 Beaver Street—space in which to study the Scriptures, pray, and have fellowship near Wall Street.

In the ensuing weeks, Barry announced that the Lord brought "the ideal couple" to run this new ministry: B.J. and Sheila Weber. I will never forget the moment that B.J. walked into Barry's office. I heard a Voice as plain as day in my mind say, "This is the guy you are going to pray for, and the guy you are going to support." Except for the months when I've failed to, I've prayed for and supported B.J. ever since (and my wife Allison has readily joined me). I was taken aback to learn that the ministry (by then legally "the New York Fellowship") did not pay B.J. or Sheila a salary. The special grant did not include monies for salaries.

My impression was . . . here is B.J. in New York City, with a new wife, and he has absolutely no assurance that funds will be available to meet their needs. I was blown away. Walking by faith is one of B.J.'s greatest strengths. I can't imagine anyone but Sheila being able to thrive like she does under these circumstances.

In the mid-1980s, I found no one needed to be a "Christian" to be accepted, culturally, into the social life of New York City—at least in Manhattan, no one expects you to be a "Christian," or go to church, etc. It seemed back then that hardly anyone did—in fact, it was reported that only three percent of the population attended church on a regular basis.

So the few Christians who became front and center in NYC became my best friends—the Thursday morning group near Wall Street and friends from Calvary-St. George's Episcopal Church. I came to realize they were like the front lines of the Body of Christ in NYC. People like the late LeGrand Jacob Ahlers, Jr. and his now widow Cynthia (left alone to raise 4 kids), Pam and Barry Abell, Bob and Tina Muzikowski, Brennan Gaertner, Daryl and Glenda Murray, Doug and Jill Dunn, Brad and Lynn Curl, Father William and Susan Wilson, Annabelle and Billy Bru, Rich and Allison Boughrum, and many more. Many of them have stories in this book!

Along with B.J and Sheila, this group of friends loved each other dearly, not to be noticed, or to be made an example, but just because of our mutual calling, affection, and love of Jesus. B.J. ministered to me personally in deep ways. I had a girlfriend from law school when I first moved to the city. B.J. came to know her and therefore wondered out loud why I was not moving forward. B.J. suggested I attend a group he put together for guys who struggled with making a commitment. It was awful. I ran out of there after the first meeting and never returned. It scared me. Well, when this girl ended our relationship, she was very kind about it and explained that I needed to get some help. Being in denial, I conveniently denied that.

I left NYC in 1988 and dated someone else (engaged for six weeks) who was not good for me. I really hit the wall. When I called B.J.

asking for $14,000 for some fancy Christian counseling, he yelled into the phone:

"Do you know how many orphans we could feed at Father William's orphanage in Bolivia with $14,000? No. I will call you right back."

B.J. sent me to the Iowa monastery, where in 1973 upon a casual visit, he had first come to faith. I met with Father Mathias, B.J.'s first mentor and close friend. I was treated like a prince.

Father Mathias sat in a chair as I sat on the floor. We prayed and prayed and prayed the name of Jesus. I started to feel a Presence, as if the Lord was in front and I was facing his back. I was still on the floor. Each time I confessed a sin, Father Mathias suggested I push the sin into the back of the Presence in front of me. I found myself pushing my awful sins into the stripes of Jesus's back while Father Mathias read aloud from Isaiah 53. Words can't describe what that was like, and I won't try.

A couple of years after the monastery "visit," I was telling B.J. about Allison Jones. Allison worked on Young Life staff and was putting herself through Fuller Seminary by working at a lobbying organization. She was beautiful, smart, had a deep faith, and adored the teenage girls she was discipling. B.J. yelled into the phone: *"I'm coming down to D.C. right away. Don't make any moves until I meet Allison."*

B.J. approved of her, after a 3-or 4-hour beer and pizza fest at a restaurant in D.C. By the way, I sat mostly at a different table because B. J. was interested in getting to know Allison.

On July 3, 1994, B. J. Weber married us in a 400-year-old Episcopal church in Charles County, Maryland. After the beautiful service, we had our reception on the eastern shore of the Potomac River, a couple of hours south of Washington, D.C. We had one of the greatest wedding exits of all time as Allison's father's ocean-going sailing vessel (named "ALLIDORO" for Allison) literally sailed us off into the sunset as we waved goodbye to all our guests.

Five years into our marriage, B.J. insisted Allison and I attend The Marriage Retreat, which helped us enormously. We continue to use these principles in our marriage today.

Allison is a rock-star. In 1998 our first daughter was born, and then our second and third daughters were born at home, with Allison not taking as much as a Tylenol because she said, "I don't want to miss a thing!" For many years, Allison has been a part-time pastor and is now in the finishing stages of her Doctorate in Divinity. The stories of connections and friendships through B.J. and Sheila Weber are endless. But what matters most, is when I have needed help, I can count on B.J. to show up and get really involved in my life, relationships, and decision making. At times there was no one better I could count on to tell it to me straight, with compassion and loving care.

Bill Lundeen is an attorney and retired partner of Ernst & Young LLP.

From Behind the Iron Curtain

By Ivan Sotirov

What has always impressed me about B.J. is his reach. He was present throughout New York's Christian community and his ministry, the New York Fellowship, was partnering with ministries throughout the nation and around the world.

When I met B.J., he was leading morning Bible study groups near the New York Stock Exchange and Rockefeller Center, and he was first on the scene to share the Christian message with United Nations ambassadors and senior staff from formerly communist countries.

When the Berlin Wall came down in the fall of 1989, B.J. and his wife Sheila organized a massive Thanksgiving dinner and invited all the U.N. ambassadors, especially focusing on those from countries formerly in the Soviet bloc, to share the true meaning of the American holiday, with its spiritual roots of gratitude to God from those who had come to Plymouth Rock for the purpose of religious freedom. Several hundred people attended, with 88 countries represented, in a luxury hotel ballroom near the U.N.

The Eastern European diplomats had not been able to attend such types of American events until the Soviet leader Mikhail Gorbachev enacted reforms and extended a new policy of "glasnost" (meaning openness) to his nation and those countries like mine behind the Iron Curtain.

I was a U.N. diplomat from Bulgaria, and this was the first time my wife and I could socialize with Americans, which led to the opportunity for a private dinner in the Weber's home. It was at their dinner table with a dozen U.N. colleagues that a prayer shook me to the core and changed my life.

Everyone shared what he or she had read in the Bible recently. When my turn came, I had to confess that because of my work in the Bulgarian U.N. Mission, I was so busy that I had not read the Bible. However, I was very glad that my wife Violet (who died a few years later) had studied the Bible diligently and shared its meaning with me.

Over dinner B.J. looked me in the eye and asked, "Ivan, do you understand that Jesus deals with each of us individually? Do you understand that Jesus died for your sins, too?" I said, "Yes, I do, but somehow I don't feel ready." To which his wife Sheila probed a bit and discovered that I meant I did not feel "good enough" yet. She explained that none of us are good enough, and that is the wonderful news of God's grace (unmerited favor) toward us. Christ has paid the price on our behalf and forgives us if we simply reach out and accept Him as Lord.

B.J. led with more explanation, and Sheila asked if I would like to say a prayer right then to receive Christ. So I bowed my head and repeated the words that she recited. At first, it was a bit mechanical feeling, but then I was gripped by the powerful words and emotion, laying my life at the feet of the Lord Jesus Christ. The others, too, felt the power of the prayer and the emotion, and congratulated me.

With B.J.'s help, I started studying the Bible, went to Christian events, and began to share my testimony. I was baptized (my first time) in the Bulgarian Orthodox church.

After a period of spiritual growth, B.J. introduced me to Ron Nikkel, the president of Prison Fellowship International, who was looking for a candidate to fill the position of Director for Prison Ministries in Eastern Europe and the former Soviet Union. Encouraged by B.J., I presented myself, and I joined the global Christian ministry founded by Chuck Colson, where I served prisoners with the message of grace and forgiveness throughout Europe for more than 20 years.

Ivan K. Sotirov was former Deputy Permanent Representative to the Permanent Mission of Bulgaria to the United Nations. With his skills in four languages, he served as former Regional Envoy for Eastern Europe and Central Asia at Prison Fellowship International.

N.Y. Yankee Baseball Chapel

By Kevin Maas

I first met B.J. when he was the leader of Baseball Chapel for the New York Yankees in 1990. It was my Rookie year in the Bronx playing for the Bombers and my faith in Jesus Christ was keeping me grounded during a record-breaking home run streak, because of which I was being pulled in many directions by fans, media, sponsors, friends, etc. The temptations and distractions in NYC were everywhere.

Our Sunday Yankee games were at 1 p.m. and therefore players were not able to attend traditional Sunday morning church service. Baseball Chapel stepped into this "church" role each Sunday game day for both home and visiting players. It is a terrific international ministry that appoints chapel leaders throughout Major and Minor League Baseball. Baseball Chapel's vision is to see players committed to their Christian faith use their platform to influence people around the world to become followers of Jesus Christ. B.J.'s life serving Christ made him a perfect fit to be the Yankee's Baseball Chapel leader. The team's 20-25 minute "chapel" sessions throughout my career were held in various places wherever we could get a little quiet time at the ballpark, which could mean sometimes in the dugout, in the showers, bullpen, or even in the stands. In Yankee Stadium, chapel was usually held in the team weight room before or after batting practice. When we finished our chapel, B.J. would share with the Visiting Team players while we were on the field for batting practice. Players would come to the weight room to hear and learn from B.J. sharing scripture, stories, and life applications. Sometimes only 4-5 attended and other times 10 or more. Most importantly, B.J. had the respect of players because he showed genuine concern for them and was authentic and unafraid when sharing his own spiritual journey, including both struggles and victories.

Baseball Chapel was just the beginning of my friendship with B.J. It was easy to want to spend more time with him outside of just our chapel sessions because he showed genuine interest in me. I knew he wanted to see me grow and stay grounded in Christ. When the team was playing home games and not traveling, B.J. would reach out to invite me to breakfast, lunch, or dinner. Sometimes we'd have one-on-one time and other times he would introduce me to Christian friends over dinner at his house. He even set me up on a blind date back in the day. That didn't work out, but hey, I appreciated the effort! After our time together, I always walked away challenged and "fed" by his wisdom, encouragement, and love for me.

One of the darkest times in my life was during my divorce many years ago. I leaned on B.J. often and phone calls to him in NYC from my home in California were so helpful, hopeful, and encouraging at a time when I was at the lowest point in my life. I never thought I would find myself in that situation, struggling through a divorce. B.J. and I would pray together on the phone not infrequently, and when traveling back to NYC for business, vacations with kids, or Old Timer's Day, I would occasionally spend a night or two with B.J. at his house and come away feeling renewed, restored, and hopeful again because B.J. has this wonderful gift of seeing and sharing Christ in all things.

B.J.'s influence in my life started with Baseball Chapel. Nearly 30+ years later, the friendship remains, and the lessons he taught are still with me. I am blessed to have a few strong, solid, committed Christian retired Major League Baseball "teammates," and I consider B.J. on that list. He lives his life to be an example for many of how much Christ loves us and he is a great example for me to see how to live a life of mercy and grace to all.

Kevin Maas played in Major League Baseball for five years. He is currently a Vice President and Certified Financial Planner at Charles Schwab in California.

N.Y. Yankees and Marriage Restoration

By Vicki Rose

In 1989, I met B.J. and Sheila Weber at a Bible study at the DeMoss House on East 73rd Street in New York. At the time, I was a brand-new believer, having surrendered my life to Jesus Christ at the Waldorf Astoria Hotel at a black-tie dinner hosted by Nancy DeMoss. And for the previous three years, I had been separated from my husband of 12 years. Our two children were seven and five years old.

The folks at the DeMoss House had told me about B.J.—that he was a minister and worked with difficult marriage cases and all kinds of people. I was very glad to meet him and his wife.

About a year later, while attending church with my husband, from whom I was still separated as we were in the throes of trying to put our marriage back together, B.J. was the guest preacher. During the sermon, I remembered that B.J. worked with and counseled struggling marriages. I leaned over and told Billy, I think we could speak to this guy and he would help us.

Billy called B.J. and they met. God truly orchestrated this meeting between my husband, a partial-owner of the Yankees baseball team, and B.J., the chaplain for the New York Yankees (during the championship years, I might add). Billy began meeting with B.J. regularly and then we met with B.J. as a couple. Our marriage needed so much help—we had so many issues—and B.J. offered us limitless time. And he never charged us a penny.

With B.J. and Sheila's wise, godly, and Biblical counsel, and after 5.5 years of separation, Billy came home, and our marriage was reconciled. Billy and I just celebrated our 42nd wedding anniversary. Over the last 28 years, there have been many bumps in the road, and B.J. and Sheila have been there to walk beside us with prayers and wise guidance, and most of all, sincere friendship and love. We praise God for this miracle and thank B.J. for walking with us through life.

Vicki Rose is a Bible teacher, conference speaker, and author of *EVERY REASON TO LEAVE: And Why We Chose to Stay Together*, released by Moody Publishers in 2014.

Bringing Heart to the NFL

By Leo Wisniewski

I first met B.J. when I was a rookie defensive lineman playing for the Baltimore Colts in 1982. We met as he was leading the NFL chapel at our team hotel near Shea Stadium, where we came to play the New York Jets. I was a young Christian, having given my life to the Lord while at Penn State in 1980. I was loved and accepted by my huddle brothers there and my life was taking off in a whole new direction following Christ.

As our NFL chapel speaker, to say that B.J. was unconventional would be a massive understatement. Most of our speakers gave us far too much sensitivity and respect. At that chapel I remember him saying something like, "God is not impressed with your talent or your celebrity. He doesn't need your money or your platform. What he IS after is your heart! He sent his son Jesus to conquer sin and death to win your heart back to him and unite you with the body of Christ in the world." He talked about the Gospel's call to lay down your life in following Jesus to serve the poor. He challenged us that as men we needed to repent from our sh*t and from our indifference to suffering all around us and the shallowness of our love. He focused on our fierce self-reliance, and how desperately we needed Christian community, not information. He shared from Jesus's Sermon on the Mount: "Blessed are the poor in spirit, for theirs is the kingdom of heaven." B.J. offered himself in friendship to me as we talked after the chapel service. Something told me this was an offer from a "rabbi" from whom I could really learn. That offseason I connected with B.J. in New York City and we became friends on a heart level. I was so encouraged by his vulnerability and playful personality.

In subsequent years, I would travel with B.J. and Father William, and often other NFL players, to many places including the Amistad Mission in Bolivia and retreats at the monastery in Iowa. At times they were the most joyful experiences, and at other times our visits together were marked by the godly sorrow that leads to true repentance. The latter gave me the gift of tears, as B.J. would remind me. At the closing of our times, my soul would be filled again with the love of Christ, the mystery of his indwelling presence in my heart, and our shared union as Christ's body in the world.

It is always fun to be with B.J., and it has always been an "iron sharpening" time. Getting involved in the New York Fellowship with him was formative in my young life as a disciple. B.J. lives out Jesus's command to his disciples: "A new command I give you. Love one another as I have loved you. By this love all men will know that you are my disciples." His cadre of brothers all over the world are marked by how they prioritize their love for one another so that the Gospel can be preached with power and relevance. He continually stresses that being an "attraction" for the Gospel must come before "promotion."

Whether we talk over the phone or meet for a weekend, times with B.J. are always filled with laughter and challenging instruction. The Proverbs say, "Iron sharpens iron, so one man sharpens another." His life ups the ante for all of us due to his deep passion for reaching men. His boldness is legendary too. He is boldly merciful and he is boldly confrontational—speaking words of mercy to those who are broken or tough words of truth to the proud.

I have been a recipient on both sides in my 37 years as his younger brother and friend. Whether I needed an "ass kicking" or a merciful confessor, B.J. brought what was needed.

I am a far better husband, father, and grandfather because of his friendship to me. There are lasting results in my life—my son Stefen Wisniewski was Collegiate All American and Academic at Penn State and has played center and guard in the NFL for nine years, including with the Super Bowl Champion Eagles. But most importantly, Stef has been integrally involved with Christian fellowship that is so prevalent throughout the NFL. I now lead a men's ministry in Pittsburgh involving several hundred guys, and I am a far better man, friend, brother in faith, and leader because of B.J.'s friendship to me.

Leo Wisniewski is the director for Locking Arms Men, a men's ministry in the Pittsburgh area whose mission is to build authentic men who love God, love one another, and love their neighbor. While at Penn State, Leo was named the Most Outstanding Defensive Player at the 1982 Fiesta Bowl and at the Hula Bowl. He was drafted #28 overall in the 1982 NFL Draft. He played four years in the NFL and was named to the 1982 NFL All-Rookie Team. He finished with the Indianapolis Colts in 1985. Knee injuries forced an early retirement. He earned a Master of Arts in Religion from Trinity School for Ministry and is a frequent speaker at men's events, churches, and retreats both in Western Pennsylvania and across the country.

Wall Street

By Vernon Outlaw

I first met B.J. in late 1991 when I was introduced to the Wall Street Bible Study he ran along with Barry Abell. After coming to Christ in January 1990 and attending an Executive Men's Bible study in Madison, N.J. for more than a year, I began attending B.J. and Barry's study since it was down the street from work. My first impression of B.J. was that he was authentic, really real, and would "tell it exactly as it was," even if it was a tad outside of decorum. Learning about his early years in ministry, this "city kid" (me) found a real connection with this minister who cut his teeth on the streets of New York City.

The connection that we found early on opened the door to wonderful opportunities that we could walk into together, beginning with his ministry to me personally. The candid conversations we had in my early years of faith helped solidify the foundation that was developing in me; that investment made it possible for Beej to challenge me to step out and step up in my faith.

The first challenge occurred when I poked at Beej to cut down the Yankee stories in the beginning of our study time. I remember saying, "Love hearing the stories, but I'm getting up early to come here for The Word." I was presented with the "funny you should mention that" response, and the next thing I knew the door opened for me to be challenged in preparing studies for the group—which went on for years. Certainly, that experience was foundational in what has become a significant portion of my ministry. From that base, our growing relationship continued to strengthen as we found wonderful opportunities to care for others, particularly in our shared heart for inner-city youth. Whether connecting with kids and their families through The East Harlem Little League or contributing to efforts to reach youth in Philadelphia and Green Bay along with Reggie White, the Beej brotherhood continued to both stretch and feed me.

B.J.'s most impactful attribute, in my opinion, and a thread that connects all who encountered his ministry over the past forty years, is how richly he invests in relationships. From the very early days, Beej sowed the time and care required to establish the premise for accountability in our relationship. In so doing, his voice was used to speak into numerous difficult situations, and it serves as a working model that continues as part of my life and ministry today. In truth, it is the canvas on which the "legacy of influence" is painted.

Beej, I thank God for you, salute you in completing 40 years of ministry, and pray God's anointing and blessing over the many years yet to come.

> Vernon Outlaw, a graduate of Columbia University, is a Senior Vice President of Corporate Bond Sales at FTN Financial. He has served as Managing Director of Utendahl Capital Partners, was a bond trader at Salomon Brothers, and was recently ordained as an associate pastor.

True Community: Surviving Suffering

By Oliver Greeves

In the summer of 1990, I was on my way from Hong Kong, where I had lived for the previous seven years, to New York City to take up a new job in a new company. I had spent many years working for Chase Manhattan heading up Chase's Asia-Pacific Investment Bank and was now returning to work for MetLife. I had been a Christian for ten years. During this time the Lord blessed me by showing how the transformed life requires being open-minded, willing to take risks, and faithful to the teachings of the Bible. Leaving close friends behind was hard, and I wondered what lay ahead of me in New York, a city well known for toughness and the value it places on material success.

In San Francisco, I stopped to meet with a few friends over lunch. Someone told me that when I reached New York I should contact B.J. and Sheila Weber, and they gave me B.J.'s phone number. A week later I met B.J., who welcomed me to join his informal group of friends, which called itself the New York Fellowship. We found we had a lot in common. Later B.J. asked me to join the small board of the Fellowship. I realized that while B.J.'s ministry had similarities with the fellowship I had belonged to in Hong Kong, B.J. had something new to teach me. B.J.'s ministry was about God's mercy. Having come from a ministry that concentrated on better understanding the Word, I realized that God was giving me the opportunity to broaden my outlook and apply what I was learning—to see another dimension of the life to which he calls us. B.J.'s ministry has a broad and a narrow focus. His broader focus is to bring believers together in fellowship or, in other words, to become part of a Community. I am sure that his years at the monastery in Iowa played an important part in his thinking in this respect. New York Fellowship embraced men and women of every background and stage in their faith journey. I was entranced to meet so many New Yorkers of every stripe—actors, sportsmen and women, businessmen, students, diplomats and politicians, reformed criminals, and recovered alcoholics—a true cross-section of the world. We met informally around the dinner table to talk about life—sometimes at B.J.'s home, sometimes in the basement of an Italian restaurant on 33rd Street.

This ministry of inclusion and encouragement brought many people into a knowledge and experience of life in Christ. In due course, one of our number, Jim Lane, took the idea and created the New Canaan Society with chapters across the United States. When I left to live in Australia, I too took this idea on the road and that led to the formation of Bridge Street Fellowship which is modelled on B.J.'s ideas, and we now have a thriving community of men in Sydney with branches in other cities.

This was B.J.'s "broad" focus. What about his "narrow" focus? I saw this, too. B.J. has the God-given empathy and courage to get alongside people who are stricken by life's blows. This could be anything from sickness, a marriage in trouble, financial failure, loss of a job, a child into drugs, or a politician who has fallen from favor. My former business partner in Hong Kong, Alex Chu, came to New York one day with his son, Derek, a boy of 13 or 14 who came for treatment at Columbia Presbyterian Hospital. The news was dreadful, but B.J. embraced that young man's perilous situation. He found out that Derek loved basketball and, miracle of miracles, got front row tickets to a game where he introduced him to Magic Johnson, Derek's hero, who was there to watch the match. Of greater importance yet, in the weeks that followed, he introduced Derek to Jesus, who would walk with him until the end of his life soon thereafter.

B.J. had an important part to play in my life, too. My dear wife, Diane, was diagnosed with lung cancer in 1994. She was not a believer at that time; however, during her protracted illness she did come to faith. The Lord took her to be with Him less than two years after her diagnosis. B.J. was one of the people who walked with her on that sad journey and B.J. and Sheila were there with me until a few minutes before she died. They continued to be my friend in the months which followed when my daughters and I tried to put our lives back together. Two years later they introduced me to Susanne to whom I am now married. B.J. conducted the wedding one lovely October day in New Hampshire when the fall leaves turned to gold. Annie was born a while later, and B.J. and Sheila have continued to be close friends even though we have lived on the other side of the world since 2004.

B.J. taught me that to be a follower of Christ means having a heart for his people and for anyone who is suffering or broken. He has taught me that the Christian life is lived in Community in which each of us has a role to play. The Lord has blessed him with a wonderful wife and family, a home in New York City, and a ministry that he describes as "retail" Christianity—by which he means he ministers through one-on-one relationships. Nevertheless, it is among the most strategic and far-reaching ministries that I have encountered.

Dr. Oliver Greeves was Asian Regional Director for Chase Manhattan's investment banking business and subsequently President of Asia Pacific for MetLife. After moving from New York City to Australia, he became a Senior Partner at the Pharos Institute, where he provides executive coaching as a rewarding complement to his career in finance and business.

The Soap Opera Actor

By Anonymous

Themes room was closing in on me. I was completely manic as the emptiness of my life and the things I chased completely collapsed on me. My God was fame and the adulation that it promised. Those hopes were built on lies and my own self-deception, but that didn't stop me. I was spiritually dead, espousing the name of Christ in concept only. I was God—the beast was my ego. I needed and demanded constant attention. Someone once said, "Adulation is like cotton candy. It tastes great but leaves your stomach empty." I reached the desolate end of adulation, starving for truth. As B.J., my brother in Christ, would say many years later, "Your persona had to be blown up in a million pieces before you could find God."

The day I met B.J., I was at the studio in midtown Manhattan. I was in my dressing room, staring in the mirror of my abyss—the deep, dark hole of my soul. I was in the middle of having a panic attack and on enough medication to take down a rhino. Then . . . the knock on the door . . . that changed my life.

There was B.J.! No. He was not wearing a cape that day, but he was riding a simple bike. B.J. rode his bike from his office at the New York Fellowship and came to hold my hand and love me—the stranger I was, referred by a mutual friend.

I'll never forget B.J.'s first words as he stared into my blood-shot, tired eyes and all their despair. He said, "Are you the actor?" I said, "Yes, I am." He studied me a moment more and said, "Really? Can't believe you're an actor. You're not even that good-looking." That always gets a laugh when I imitate B.J. I say imitate. There is no other B.J. He is an odd mix of Bill Murray on steroids and George C. Scott—irreverent yet so commanding. B.J. is not showy or drowning in pretense. He entered my life with complete transparency, wearing his own humanity and vulnerabilities like a loose piece of clothing. It is not dogma that drives B.J. but the revealing of the authentic love and humanity of Christ. He walked into my life with that love and compassion of the Christ he loves so. He talked to me that day for about an hour. I listened as intently as a broken person could and was mesmerized by the simple truths of God's love for me. I was completely mystified! Who does this sort of thing? Nobody in the church I knew, that's for sure. When B.J. was done, I grabbed my checkbook and I said, "How much do I owe you for your visit?" He told me to put my checkbook away— I could pay him back by being available once a week. (Excuse me!)

"See ya, Brother," he proclaimed. Then as quickly as he arrived, off B.J. went on his magic bike. Hmm.

What just happened to me? As I reflect, I'm reminded of the man who arrived humbly in Jerusalem on a donkey to change the world. B.J. entered my life on a beat-up bike. I experienced the true meaning of church and the fullest embodiment of Christ's love that day.

I've been blessed to be sober almost seven years by the grace of God, Alcoholics Anonymous (AA), and my beloved brother, B.J. The first step of AA is "I'm powerless over alcohol and my life has become unimaginable." B.J. guided me to this idea of surrendering my ego but also making it OK not to be the perfect Christian. B.J. knows the Pharisees and destroys their lies with the agape love of Christ. When the church turned its back on me, B.J. shared this prophetic truth: "There is nothing wrong with God except God's people."

What amazing wisdom, grace, and mercy from the Iowa rugby player who wandered into a monastery and became Christ's disciple. I'm so blessed to have B.J. as a friend. I love him more than words can bring justice here.

Ernest Hemingway wrote, "The world breaks everyone and some are stronger in their broken places." B.J. entered my broken place with a love not of this world, but of the Christ Jesus. Thank you B.J.!

This writer was an Emmy-nominated actor on one of the most popular shows on television. In addition, he recently became an award-winning playwright. He requested to remain anonymous and honor the traditions of the 12-step program in regard to press, radio, and film.

My Surprising Columbia University Rugby Coach

By Kern Collymore

B.J. Weber is an amazing human being who has taught me so much. When I first met B.J. I was in my junior year at Columbia University. At the time, I couldn't imagine the role he would play in my life. I was raised in a traditional Catholic, Caribbean household, but found myself moving away from religion during my high school years. After getting accepted to Columbia University, I played collegiate football for the next two years. After my sophomore year I took a year off from school; when I returned, all my football friends were playing rugby. I had to check it out. B.J. was our rugby coach. For months I was able to learn rugby under his guidance and saw our rugby team go from 0-8 to 5-3 in one season. That year our team went to Argentina, and it was also an opportunity to see B.J. in a light that really allowed me to respect the person he was.

When I was growing up, I found myself amongst a lot of judgmental "religious" people. However, I never got that sense from B.J. I had earlier met a lot of "Christians" who said and did things that I felt did not fall in line with Christianity. Meeting B.J. was refreshing because at that point I did not know many Christians who practiced their faith the way B.J. does. I spent months on the rugby team before I found out that "Coach B.J." was actually a pastor! While on tour, I was able to see his compassion as he often went out of his way to help people. I observed his passion, as he was ready to defend those under his care. And I saw his ability to live in the moment, which to me was very surprising for a pastor.

I have always been grateful for the way B.J. has the ability to make people feel seen, but more than that, he is able to be vulnerable without putting up facades. I remember being in college and having conversations with B.J. about his son Max and how much love he had for him, which made me deeply analyze my relationship with my own father. If Max was having a difficult time, it was obvious how much it affected B.J. He was able to have an open conversation with us and he was always open to learning new things and hearing new perspectives that were different from his own.

Most people help others based on what they are able to get in return, but not B.J. Since meeting B.J., he has helped me in so many ways with no expectations in return. He was able to use his connections to get me interviews in some very elite institutions, and through his connections I eventually landed a job at the Buckley School after graduating. Little did I know that that would just be the beginning of my story with B.J.

Soon after starting at Buckley, my partner and I found out we were pregnant. For most of her life she had been told that she would not be able to bear a child, so when she found out she was pregnant, she was elated. But we were scared at the thought of being married, or even being formally a "couple." B.J. was able to provide us with counseling, talking to us about the importance of being a family unit when raising a child. That spring my pregnant fiancé and I were able to go to Trinidad on a rugby tour with B.J. and Sheila. We experienced the love they had for each other. After we had our child, B.J. was such an integral part of our life that we had our wedding in the Weber's living room. Thirty of our close friends attended the ceremony and dinner in the Weber's home. It was magical and would not have happened without B.J.'s help and support. To this day, B.J. and my son have a special relationship. I feel like B.J. is the kind of person with whom everyone feels like they have a special and unique relationship, and that is a testament to the type of man he is.

My wife and I decided to leave New York City and move back to her Navajo reservation in the Southwest. Thousands of miles away, B.J. still supported me anytime I needed help. He helped to fund garden projects, youth outreach, and many other community-building initiatives I've been a part of, always offering his help. I sometimes wonder what it is that he sees in me or what I did to deserve the help I've had from B.J.

As the years have passed, I have been lucky to be able to have this continued contact and relationship, most recently with B.J. visiting me in the Southwest as my wife finished up a political campaign. To see B.J. in our home, while celebrating my wife's accomplishments, brought me back to sitting in his living room as he talked to us about committing to be a strong family together. The example that B.J. sets of what it means to be a Christian has made a tremendous impact on our lives as well. Both my wife and I have had negative experiences in the church and have seen what feels like hypocrisy of "faith-based" organizations (e.g., competitiveness about theology and attendance), but B.J. has been such a positive influence in our lives that when we talk about Christians we designate them into "judgmental Christians" (not grace-filled) and the other group we refer to as "B.J. Christians," and fortunately we have met more of those through his friendship.

Kern Collymore is the founder of Dine Climb, located in Navajo Nation, Arizona, which brings climb training to indigenous youth and activists working on environmental and social justice issues. He and his wife are co-founders of Sixth World Solutions, where they help Navajo communities implement sustainable solutions through local governance policies and pursue economic development in sustainable industries.

Rescuing our Ivy League Child

By the Anonymous Parents

"Remember that we deal with alcohol—cunning, baffling, powerful! Without help it is too much for us. But there is One who has all power—that One is God. May you find Him now!"
– The Big Book of Alcoholics Anonymous

When we met with B.J., we were in a battle for our child and our family. Alcohol and addiction—with all their cunning, baffling, and powerful ways—were winning. The first thing B.J. did was to explain in clear and direct terms just how much danger we were in. B.J. also gave us hope. With many years of experience serving others in 12-Step programs, he spoke with authority about the transformative potential of this work, not only for our child but for each of us, for our marriage, and for our other children. He also reminded us—often—that Almighty God was with us, even though we felt confused, afraid, and powerless.

Nothing happened quickly. There were setbacks and disappointments. B.J. helped us think through difficult decisions for our child's treatment and also kept us focused on our own recovery. We made the drastic choice to withdraw our child from an elite university. Thankfully, we can report that our child embraced recovery, successfully graduated, and is doing well today. As we think back now, one thing that sustained us in the darkest times was B.J.'s courage. He was steadfast and loving, and we knew he was fighting with us. His example is always with us and has helped us to encourage other parents in similar situations.

The authors, both mother and father, have had successful professional careers in New York City. They are honoring their child's anonymity, in alignment with AA's credo, while offering their heartfelt appreciation to B.J.

Jesus Wept (N.Y. Fellowship newsletter following 9/11)

By B.J. Weber

September 20, 2001

Dear friends,

I do not know what to tell you or what to say. Everything seems so trifling. I have a difficult time praying. Sleep is irregular at best. A week after the bombings, the most common emotion is a deep, deep sadness. Yesterday before I had my coffee, I wept three times. After the second day a film of ash covered our backyard and porch, a reminder of the inferno and holocaust just a few miles from our home.

It's a horror beyond one's imagination. (And Jesus wept.) Trying to be useful, I spend my days at the "bereavement center" at the Armory, only a few blocks from our home. Thousands of people line up, filling out missing person reports describing their loved ones, and collapsing under the weight of the reality that their loved ones would not be found. Asking for DNA material/dental charts was perhaps the most difficult of my tasks. Tearfully, they know that rescue was not possible and recovery remote.

New York stories abound. A Muslim woman lost three family members and she asked me, "Is your God a God of love?" I prayed with her and told her that Jesus was also the God of life as well as love. A Hispanic woman who lost her husband has three kids to support. She buckled under the grief and sorrow that lay before her. A medical doctor gave her a Benadryl. She fell into my arms and responded, "I don't need drugs, I need God and prayer." A family from Jamaica lost a son/brother. I spent three hours listening to their sadness as they came to grips with their worst fears. After we prayed together the mother invited me to their home for "real Jamaican food." A new friend. (And Jesus wept.) The stories are legion: family friend Tom Duke was on the 105th floor of the second tower and he and a handful of colleagues showed up at our door in shock—they had survived. However, 60 of their company were unaccounted for: family friends, little league sponsors, good and gracious people gone and unaccounted for. Father Michael Judge, chaplain for the fire department and co-laborer in Christ, died with his men.

Except for the sirens which blare day and night, the city is amazingly quiet. Cars don't honk their horns; people are eerily silent and stunned. Generosity and graciousness abound. People stop and comfort others, flags fly everywhere, but a subtle hope is beginning to emerge.

Two cops, sitting in their cruiser, were weeping. I offered to pray with them, and they offered me a ride home. Heroes everywhere: 343 firefighters are dead as well as 60 cops and death has not abated. We received hundreds of phone calls, many concerned wives and many seeking news of loved ones. Dutifully, I would scan the DOA list and hospital lists in hopes of finding news of lost family members and friends. It's a horror.

My children are struggling. Max's hands were shaking at school and he has lost many nights' sleep. Rachel's close friend's mother is still missing. Rachel spent September 12th at her friend's home, calling hospitals in the search effort, then fell into bed after bouts of nausea. That same night, our neighborhood was evacuated from a bomb threat to the Empire State Building nearby. Just as Sheila was deciding to pull the children out of bed and head to the East River, the police sounded the all clear. The following day Grand Central Station was evacuated—where our children must pass twice a day to and from school. The trauma became even more real to us.

Acts of heroism and generosity are commonplace. People from around the world have shown tremendous love and support. One of the biggest needs is temporary housing. Tens of thousands are displaced. It's a horror. And Jesus wept. Personally, we are inconsolable. We are trying to help and serve, but the truth is the funerals have not yet begun.

Thank you for your loving responses, concern, prayers, and friendship. It is our calling to be in New York City during the nation's and city's hour of sorrow—September 11, 2001—a day that will be our generation's "Day of Infamy." People are open to the Lord as we've never seen in all our 23 years here. Please continue to pray.

In Christ's service,

B.J. Weber

Home Base

By Max Weber

Imagine the most perfect day. It was the first day of school. I was an upper-classman now, with college on the horizon, and the weather was perfect—the type of weather that no matter what you wear, you're comfortable. I was excited to see my friends after the summer vacation, our whole lives open before us. We were 16 or 17 years old; we thought we knew everything we needed to know, but the teachers were acting funny . . . not their jovial selves. They did not have that first day of school buzz. Then the headmaster got on the video announcement system. Strange . . . he never gave video announcements. We were making fun of him. He looked sloppy, and he bumped into the camera. He stumbled over his words. Then the reality of his announcement started sinking in. Is this a joke? Is this a dream? It didn't add up. Some of us older kids left school and ran to the corner of the avenue to look downtown; we had to see it with our own eyes. We had to see these two great giants that always seemed to loom over us, protecting our city, ever watching over us. They could be seen from almost everywhere and it was true, they were on fire. Then there was only one of them; then they were both gone.

All of the kids were eventually ushered back into school and everything was put on lock down. Cell phone technology was a newer concept; plenty of kids had them but none of them were working. We were told that none of us were allowed to leave without a parent or guardian escort. The reality sunk in that we might be here a long time. How would I get back to my family at home base about forty blocks away? Our joyous first day of school had just been canceled. What about the kids' parents who worked down there? In other boroughs or Jersey? We were told our parents had been notified and we had to sit tight. I could not tell you if it was 30 minutes or eight hours, but my father finally showed up on a bicycle. My first words to him were, "Dad, is this real?" His grave words back to me were, "Son, this is very real, as real as it gets." He quickly explained that most of the city's transportation had been shut down, so he and my mother had taken two bicycles and had gone to pick up me and my sister, who was at another school. There was an announcement on TV that school kids had to be picked up in person. My father picked me up because I was across town and further away. So, I gave my backpack to my father and I ran alongside his bicycle. Adrenaline pumping, I could have run for days. At 16 years old, captain of my varsity sports teams, testosterone pumping through my veins, with nothing but the silence of NYC and the sound of my footsteps, I felt alone with my thoughts as we ran across Central Park to the predetermined meeting spot my parents had agreed upon. We finally ran into my sister and mother and one of my sister's friends whom she had known since she was four years old; she was coming home with us that afternoon. We were walking down Fifth Avenue with my mother holding a bicycle. My sister's friend's mother worked on the 99th floor of the World Trade Center.

We all put on brave faces and showed only optimism. I needed to get back to home base and then I would devise the next steps. My father could see rash teenage angst behind my eyes and told my mother to give me her bike because we were going to go do something. We did not know quite what, but we would think of a plan on the way. The further and further south we biked, the more and more crowded the avenues became. People were covered in soot, tears streaming down their faces, and besides the occasional siren, there was complete and utter silence. It was an eerie silence you would only understand if you experienced it. There is constant noise at all times when you are in midtown Manhattan. I had never heard it so silent. Cars were not moving. No one honked. The streets were a parking lot. Subways were closed. Thousands of people were flooding the streets, walking home in utter silence. Even the birds were silent. It felt like a war zone.

We decided to see if we could donate blood. There had to be thousands of people who needed it. When we got to NYU hospital, the line to give blood was around the block. So many people showed up to give blood, they turned everyone away who was not O-positive or O-negative. My father and I waited and waited because we both happened to be O-positive. Even still, the line was too long. We decided to go home and think of another plan. On our way home, my father saw a meter maid giving people tickets. My father could not believe it. He told her that this was the biggest disaster the city had ever seen! How could someone be expected to move their car? Once we reached our home at 232 East 32nd Street, we found our steps filled with people who were covered in soot. They were my father's friends who could not get home. It turns out that 232 wasn't just my home base. That day it became home base for a number of people—a true refuge in the middle of what seemed like the end of the world. My father and mother, of course, took everyone in and we knew our role was to comfort and help the people around us. We could only pray that our loved ones throughout the country knew we were safe, because by this time cell phone service in New York City had been shut off.

My best friend whom I have known since kindergarten (we were best men in each other's weddings) went to a different high school, and he, too, could not get home; so of course he showed up at home base—our house. So many people spent the night that night. So much confusion, anger, sorrow, weeping, and numbness. The following day, my father got right to work; I stayed home because I could not handle any more of the pressure. My mother and sister used the landline phone to call hospital after hospital looking for my sister's friend's mother. My father went to the local firehouse to offer any help that he could. Once my father found out that the meeting place for people seeking information about their loved ones was established at the NYC Armory on East 24th street, a mere few blocks from our house, he knew where he was called to be.

Whereas I shut the world out over the next few days and weeks, my father tried to be a beacon of hope for anyone who needed it. He was granted access to Ground Zero and spent countless hours at the Armory from September 12th on. I could not tell you if it was two weeks or eight weeks, but my father barely slept. Between funerals, grief counseling, ground zero, and meeting victims' family members at the Armory and the firehouse, my father would come home every night with more tragic, grievous stories. And I was there to listen. His first day in the Armory he encountered countless frantic, screaming people jammed everywhere. There were stations set up for those looking for loved ones, grief counseling, therapy, but at first there were no priests or religious or spiritual guidance of any kind. My father put on his clerical collar and set up a sign that said: "Can I pray with you?" The line of people wrapped around the block to seek counsel. They wept with my father, who often held them, dozens upon dozens of strangers who he never saw again. In those early weeks after 9/11, my father would spend sometimes 15 to 20 hours a day away from home, between hours at the firehouse, the Armory, helping with a funeral, with widows and orphans, time at Ground Zero, or in private counsel. The only people who knew he was going to the Armory were his immediate family. I know my father was not sleeping at night, even in the few hours he had off. He would come to home base to recharge, even if he couldn't sleep. In our Christmas card that year, my father looked like Dracula or a ghost.

On September 12th school was canceled, and we all seemed to have to fend for ourselves, certainly emotionally. While my sister and mother called hospital after hospital looking for hope, and my father did all that he could to help, I could not emotionally get past my anger and confusion. I was ready to fight. I had to take a step back. So, as I was alone, I decided the only thing I could do was try to escape and I went to the movies. Shockingly the theater was open. I asked the ticket teller which was a comedy and she sold me a ticket to the movie Rat Race. I was the only person in the theater and to this day this movie holds a special place in my heart. To me, a 16-year-old, filled with indescribable emotions, all alone, I proceeded to laugh to tears for the following two hours. I cried with laughter, fell out of my seat, no one was there to share it with me. When I left the theater, I felt like a million bucks, back to my innocence. I practically skipped home with a grin still on my face. I was going up my front steps when I noticed something was off. Midtown New York City in the middle of the day was eerily quiet. Then the tidal wave that was reality hit me in the gut. 9/11 was yesterday. A date that won't be forgotten for generations. It is my generation's December 7. Was it possible I just saw a movie that made me forget 9/11 for two and a half hours?

That night there was a bomb threat in the Empire State Building just a few blocks from our house and hordes of people were being evacuated and were streaming down our street to head to the East River. The police loudspeakers shouted for us to leave our homes. At 9 p.m. my sister was emotionally wiped out and already in bed, when my mother told us to get our shoes on, that unbelievably we had to get away from our neighborhood as fast as we could. Just as we were headed out the door, the police sounded the all clear. But we lived with the stress that a bomb could go off at any moment. The next day, September 13th, school was back in session and I later blocked out a memory that I rode our bicycle to school, because the subways were either shut down or evacuated for bomb threats, and my parents thought it was safer for me to take the bike. We did not learn anything in school that day. In every class we just talked about what this meant for our future and our lives and the people who were suffering. My mother said that by the time I had ridden the bike back home after school and walked in the door, I was shaking.

That night I did something else I completely forgot until she reminded me years later. That is what trauma does, it makes you block out memories to protect you. The night of September 13th my mother and father were busy trying to help those with the most need and talking on our landline phone, which rang nonstop with folks from around the country calling to check on us. I did not seek out their counsel or guidance because I didn't want to add to their burden. At midnight, my parents had barely been able to check in with each other and were debriefing after two days of limited sleep. They were discussing how their children were handling this. In my mind they were trying to hold NYC together, yet they did not want their kids to slip through the cracks and realized that they had not checked in too deeply into how we were feeling. So, my father decided to get some much-needed rest, and my mother decided to check on my sister and me to see if either of us was still awake. As she walked up the stairs toward my room, she noticed under the door that my light was still on. She knocked gently and entered slowly, calling "Max? Are you still awake?" What she saw was surprising, but she approached with no reaction. I had dug into the backs of all my closets to my old toy bins and pulled out every action figure, army man, Lego figure with a sword, and every inch of my room was covered with army men and toys doing battle. It must have taken six hours of my time to set it up. My mother said I was deep in thought and she asked, "How are you doing?" Remember, I was nearly 17, and most teenagers stop playing with army men at age 11, but today was an exception. I did not know how to handle the emotion, so I reverted to childhood. At my mother's inquiry, I got very dark and looked down on my massive battle scene in my room and simply said, "I just want to get those guys. I just want to get them!" My mom said, "Sweetheart, why don't you stay home from school tomorrow." I nodded my head with a tear rolling down my cheek and my mother quietly closed the door. Unbeknownst to me, my mother checked in on me a few more times that night, and I stayed awake with my army men until dawn.

Over the next few weeks, I tried to at least be emotionally available for my father, but it was hard for a teenager. He would come home every day with horribly tragic new stories. One of the early stories that stood out to me was while people were waiting in line to pray with him at the Armory, there was a woman in line dressed in a hijab, and my father was certainly surprised and welcomed her to pray. She wept in his arms and neither of them cared about religious stigmas. She told my father that her husband worked in the restaurant on the 110th floor of the WTC. She cried, "He was my husband, our breadwinner, our everything. What are we supposed to do without him? Do you think he made it out safely? Do you think that is a possibility?" My father prayed and wept with her, and tried to give her hope that maybe he found a way down past the flames. None of us yet knew how absolute the destruction was. My father said they could meet tomorrow and look for her husband in a hospital. I became short-tempered with him and fed up with the story. "Dad, don't you see, there is no way he could have made it down from the 110th floor. It is not possible." My dad looked at me through tears and said, "There has to be! You don't think he could have found a stairwell that was not on fire? There has to be a chance!" My father's empathy has always been boundless. I tried to say it softer, but I reassured him that these attacks were final. If you were caught above, you were not making it down. My father wept the rest of the night. My 16-year-old heartless mind made a mental note that I am not built for things like this—grief counseling or empathy for others. My father had a certain emotional capacity for things I could not touch with a 10-foot pole. I realized my best way to support him was to just close my mouth and let God use my father as a vehicle of hope and comfort.

As the days bled into weeks and weeks bled into months, my father really found his calling and purpose with the local firehouse. He became their personal firehouse chaplain. Their house was hit hard. They lost nine members that day. One of their members was one of the only people to survive the actual collapse. (He is featured in a famous documentary about the small group that survived, called "The Miracle in Stairwell B.") My father ended up helping with a number of funerals and grief counseling with widows, family members, and actual survivors of that day.

We became close with one firefighter in particular named Joe Finley, whose own father had been killed in the infamous 23rd Street fire of 1966. I got to witness what the life of a firefighter looked like through our families growing close to each other. At first, I had a yearning to join the military to quell my intense need for justice and protection for our nation and our freedoms, but that matured into a love for my city and my fellow citizens at home. After observing these firefighter families, I determined that was a lifestyle that I wanted for my future.

Joe Finley ended up retiring due to 9/11 asthma and moved to Nashville, where I happened to be in college and was able to stay connected with him. I explored several different career paths, but the firefighter itch/bug would not get out of my system. Joe Finley encouraged me to apply to the FDNY. When I finally announced to my parents that was the career I wanted, no matter its humble means, I was shocked and pleasantly surprised by their reaction and support of my decision. They were so proud of me.

I currently serve as an FDNY firefighter. For years my father was involved with our family's local firehouse and helped with their 9/11 service. I have committed my life to serve and hope to continue my father's legacy. B.J. Weber is a one-man marching band filled with ideas, prospects, hopes, dreams, and love for his fellow man, and above all, a servant of Christ. I hope to do this one thing as well as my father has been able to do dozens upon dozens of works of service. I want to thank his faithful friends for their love and support in helping him spread the love and call of Jesus.

Editor's note: Through B.J.'s introductions, FDNY firefighter Joe Finley was chosen to give a short speech and Scripture reading at the National Prayer Breakfast in Washington, D.C. a few months after the 9/11 attack. At that event, Lisa Beamer, whose husband Todd courageously brought down United Airlines Flight 93 in Shanksville, Pennsylvania, also read Scripture and spoke before President Bush delivered his remarks.

Maxwell A. Weber and his wife currently live in the Washington Heights neighborhood of upper Manhattan with their children Bo (16 months old) and Lita (3 months old). Max has served in the Fire Department as an EMT since 2010 and as an FDNY firefighter since 2013. Max's wife, Lauren, was former Young Life area director in Connecticut, and former director of operations at The Geneva School in Manhattan. Max attended Vanderbilt University and helped run Chicago's Near West Little League for two summers. For the last fifteen years, Max has played for Old Blue RFC, the same NYC rugby team that his father played on years ago.

Thrown into the Deep End

By Rev. Dr. Nathan Hart

It was the summer of 2002. I had just completed my first year of Princeton Seminary when I showed up at B.J.'s office for the first day of my summer internship with the New York Fellowship. It was one of those hot Manhattan days and the window air conditioners were on their highest setting, buzzing loudly as I earnestly asked B.J. what I should expect from the internship. Sitting behind his desk, B.J. began describing a young man who was in a lot of trouble. He had gotten into some fights with gangs, was a drug and alcohol user, and worse. His uncle was a Wall Street lawyer who thought B.J. could help. I listened to B.J.'s story and felt sad for the guy. Growing up in a small town in the Midwest, I had never encountered a real-life person in this kind of trouble. But then I heard B.J. say to me, "He's going to be arriving here any minute. He's going to be *your project* for the summer."

The words *"your project"* buzzed in my head even more loudly than the air conditioners' noise. I was terrified. Minutes later, I felt even worse when the young man entered the office. I immediately noticed his large muscles protruding from a ratty tank top and a gnarly black eye on his face. (He had been hit with a baseball bat two nights prior.) He sat down and looked at B.J. and me like we were the lucky participants in his next street fight. His leg twitched and his eyes were wild.

After a few minutes of B.J. telling the young man he was loved, and the young man soundly rejecting that kind of talk, B.J. left the room. I had no idea what to do. B.J. had thrown me into the deep end of crisis counseling, pastoral care, addiction recovery, and intervention. In that moment, and for the next few weeks, I had no option but to trust God and seek his guidance for every decision. I remember having a hard time falling asleep that first night, wondering if the young man was going to leave the apartment and go into the city streets, or God forbid, walk over to my bed and try to harm me. I woke up the next morning, got some breakfast with him, and took him to an AA meeting a few blocks away.

By the end of that summer, the young man was placed safely in a rehab facility and was starting to rebuild his life. I was a changed person. Because of B.J.'s approach—that is, throwing me into the deep end—I learned things I wouldn't have otherwise learned with a "normal" summer internship. I learned the depths of God's love, the reality of the Holy Spirit's daily provision, and the saving grace of Jesus Christ, who can heal every wound by his redeeming blood and resurrection power.

I carry these lessons with me today as I serve as the senior pastor of Stanwich Church in Greenwich, CT. I am grateful for God's work through B.J. in my life.

Rev. Dr. Nathan Hart is senior pastor of the Stanwich Church in Greenwich, CT, was formerly NYC director of FOCUS (Fellowship of Christians in Universities and Schools), intern at the New York Fellowship, and clergy at Brookville Reformed Church in Long Island. He graduated from Hope College, and earned a Master of Divinity from Princeton Theological Seminary and a D.Min. from Gordon-Conwell Theological Seminary.

The Butterfly Effect

By Robert Monteleone

"Does the flap of a butterfly's wings in Brazil set off a hurricane in Texas?" asks Edward Lorenz in *The Chaos Theory*. He proposes that the "butterfly effect is the sensitive dependence on initial conditions in which a small change in one state of a deterministic nonlinear system can result in large differences in a later state."

In the summer of 2002, chaos arrived in my life like a category 3 hurricane. I was informed that a divorce was coming and that there was no way to avoid it. I was given a couple of hours to pack up my things and leave our cottage at the beach. It was suggested I stay in the New York City apartment. I packed up a couple of bags, threw them into the truck and headed home to NYC.

As I headed back to the City, I had a clear sense that this was not going to be a temporary separation. I was between panic and tears. I began pleading to God over and over, "Help me, oh dear God, please help me." I had heard it said many times before this day,

"You will not realize that God is all you need until God is all you have."

On the road the first call was to my good friend George Rose. He said, without a doubt in his mind, "Call B.J. Weber—he can help." I took down the number and called. I left a message. George called B.J. too.

As I drove toward the City, two things settled peacefully within me: first, that I needed and desired God to get through this storm, and second, that I did not want to survive this storm only to live a loveless life of bitterness and regret. I instantly committed to those two desires and decided to bypass NYC, heading straight to a Trappist Monastery in Kentucky I had been to a couple of times. God was there in Kentucky waiting for me, and He prepared me to meet B.J. Weber.

After nearly six weeks in The Abbey of Gethsemane, I returned to New York. It was September. The hurricane was now a category 4. A lawyer was threatening all kinds of havoc. I called B.J. and we met at his office at Calvary Church.

B.J.'s first words to me after hello, nice to meet you, were, "Do you mind if we pray?" Whatever had been occupying the place for prayer in my heart had just been suddenly kicked out. "Do you mind if we pray?" B.J. asked me with kindness and empathy. "We?" he asked. I had never been asked to pray with anyone. I had been told to pray, but never asked to pray. But there was another dimension I heard his words reach. The words lacked warmth, yet were still kind, like he was asking the bully riding my bike, "Do you mind if we ride the bike now?"

B.J. prayed like a prince kneeling before the King, head down, eyes away, humble, adoring, intimate, yet fearless and bold. He prayed out loud! He did not recite a prayer. He prayed like he actually knew God.

We talked for quite a while and when we finished B.J. again said, "Let's pray." It wasn't a question this time, it was The Answer! With both his hands he covered my hands. What happened next I will never ever forget, and I have told it a hundred times, and every single time I tell this story I cry. I seriously cry. B.J. began praying out loud. He was talking to God about all the things we had just talked about, all the hurt, the fear, the anger, the unknown, the unworthiness, and the desire to know Him. But what staggered me was that B.J. was talking to God about me! It was like B.J. held my hand and walked right up to the King, introduced me, and then he proceeded to tell Him my needs. I had never in my life had an advocate for my needs. B.J. cared and—most importantly—B.J. knew without a doubt that God cared more. I hadn't ever realized anyone cared about me or my needs before, but I can say this: I have never doubted someone does since that day.

I went to see and hear B.J. preach at St. George's on Sunday (part of Calvary-St. George's historic, merged churches). I do not recall the sermon; I do clearly recall B.J. introducing me to Oliver Greeves, Mark Burner, Rev. Tom Pike, and Eric Metaxas. B.J. asked Oliver and Rev. Pike if they would pray with me. I knelt and they each put a hand on my back and prayed. These men took turns praying to God, asking Him to help me the way He has helped them. No one recited anything by rote; I could feel their faith in their words, and it gave me hope that God could hear their words. Their words were my words, and because I didn't have the faith in God that they did, I could only hope He was listening to them. Before leaving, Rev. Pike asked if I would like to come by his office the next evening "to have a chat."

The next night I went to Calvary Church to "have a chat" with Tom Pike. After greetings and with coffee poured, Tom started our chat with: "Do you mind if we pray?" Tom prayed and I listened. Tom was in cleric's dress so his praying seemed less like B.J.'s freestyle prayer. However, after the prayer, Rev. Pike told me that when he was a young man, his first wife left him years ago. (He has been happily remarried for the last 40 years.) I hadn't realized that married pastors could divorce until that moment. We discussed the state of my affairs, my readiness for what lay ahead, and Tom talked of his divorce—that gave me such comfort at that time to know that if a woman divorces you, God isn't going to divorce you. We wrapped up the evening praying about the things we discussed. It staggered me again, to hear my prayers said out loud and with faith, not shame. Rev. Pike asked me to come again the next week and suggested I join Alpha, a new class for searchers that was just beginning. I went.

It was during the weeks of Alpha that I came to know Eric Metaxas. During the first weeks of Alpha, the hurricane had reached a category 5 stage and had stalled over all areas of my life; assets were frozen, bills fell behind, my son's next college tuition payment was due and the lawyers had other cases. The Alpha small groups proved to be a blessing that I would have never sought on my own. There were people who had bigger problems yet more faith than I had at the time, and there were others who had much smaller problems and virtually little faith or no desire for God. Eric introduced us to Christianity through questions and answers, reading and discussing the Bible, and praying. We read C.S. Lewis and I found his writings like Windex on the foggy window through which the Bible showed Jesus. Everything was clearer afterward. Eric gave a talk about Jeremiah 29:11: "For I know the plans I have for you," declares the LORD, "plans to prosper you and not to harm you, plans to give you hope and a future." I left with that Bible verse imbedded in me like a new outlet; that verse provided a new power source for hope. I prayed for the first time out loud, and it was to ask Him to help another man upon whose shoulder my hand had rested.

Oliver Greeves invited me to go to New Canaan Society with him for a Christian men's meeting and fellowship. We talked about losing my wife to divorce and he told about losing his wife to illness and death. He talked about his bitterness and fear of loving again. We went to Jim Lane's house and parked on the neighbor's lawn. Inside Oliver introduced me to scores of men I had not met before. Mark Burner, Rev. Pike, Eric Metaxas, and B.J. were there, too. We talked over breakfast sandwiches, sang along with the worship band. Jim Lane introduced B.J., then B.J. introduced the speaker, and then before handing the microphone to the speaker, B.J. looked out to the 80 men in Jim's living room and said, "Let's pray." A man called out his prayer for a daughter, another for work, others for their marriage or their friend's marriage, for a sick friend, and then Oliver called out a prayer for me, that I would know the loving Christ. When all the prayer requests had been made, B.J. dipped his head a bit lower, put his hand on the speaker's shoulder, and prayed for all the prayers and especially for the speaker and his words, that they would bring comfort to the suffering in the room. On the way home, Oliver talked more about the bitterness and fear of loving again, and then he went on to tell me how "The Lord" worked through Eric, Mark, Tom, and especially B.J. to lead him away from bitterness and lovelessness. His spirit soared as he told me about his older children and how happy they were that he had found love again. He told me about his new wife Suzanne (introduced to him by B.J.'s wife Sheila), and their young daughter, Annie.

B.J. encouraged me that winter to join him and the New Canaan guys on their retreat at the Mohonk Mountain House. They provided me with a scholarship. After one session, I joined a small group of men in a little room to discuss the day's session and to pray. One man who seemed to be in the inner circle of the New Canaan leadership shared a dark, dark secret with us, something that had been going on and eating him up for quite some time. He wept openly. I became uncomfortable when he curled up into the fetal position. He convulsed with tears and shame. One man went over and, without touching the writhing man, held out his open hand as if to provide the channel, before he began praying. He prayed to have the man's sin forgiven and the desire to sin removed. He prayed for a long time. I joined the other men to pray. We prayed for our own sinful desires to be removed. We prayed for a long time, too. Walking back to my room, I felt that I had just been told the truth about having faith in Christ. Sin will not walk away just because I say I am with Christ. There will be fierce efforts and secret efforts and subtle efforts to separate me from Christ Almighty. That night's discussion was on Ephesians 6:11.

The next morning at the retreat, I went cross-country skiing because B.J. refused to take no for an answer. We skied beneath the tall trees and came to a path that looked west over the hills of New York. That was the first time I had done something I had never done before that I had always wanted to do, but was afraid to do. We rested leaning on our ski poles, looking over the vast hills before us. The sky was bright and clear. I prayed quietly into a slight yet icy cold breeze. I thanked God for B.J. and that he had taught me to pray. He showed me it all begins and ends with prayer. Loving prayer.

For his leadership in its formation, there was a picture of B.J. on a plaque hanging on a wall on the 3rd floor of the Bowery Mission Men's Transitional Center on Avenue D. For whatever reason his picture has been lost, but the plaque of appreciation to him remains. When I see that plaque, I know why I volunteer there: to do what B.J. did for me. I am to show someone I care about them and to tell them that God cares about them even more than I could. I share Jeremiah 29:11. I pray with them, I pray for them, I ask them to pray for me.

Being asked to write my thoughts about B.J.'s friendship is beyond an honor; it really is a duty. However, this sense of duty is betrayed because I don't think B.J. wants to be the subject. The focus should be on what God has done.

I have struggled to paint a portrait of a man who is so like a butterfly. As Robert Frost wrote, "Butterflies...flowers that fly and all but sing."

God used B.J. as the butterfly that calmed my hurricane.

After decades finding joy in a career in the fresh seafood industry, Robert Monteleone now spends his time reading, writing, volunteering, and looking forward to seeing his three grandchildren. In 2007 he remarried, and he and his wife, Gretchen, live in NYC and the Hudson Valley.

The Intern:
Launching into the Unknown

By Tyler Slade

I still remember my first day as B.J.'s intern as if it were yesterday. B.J. wanted to walk over to his local firehouse in Midtown Manhattan because it happened to be the second anniversary of 9/11. Since the attack, he had been spending a lot of time with the firemen of that house, helping them walk through their grief. I was overwhelmed by the gravity of the situation and felt awkward and unprepared to interact with people dealing with such tragedy in their lives. But B.J. dove right in as if he weren't weighed down at all by the heaviness of the moment. He was able to be open and attentive to the men, their families, and what they were going through. I was impressed. After a while they asked B.J. to lead them in a time of prayer and remembrance. I can remember thinking, *I'm glad it's him and not me . . . I wouldn't know what to say to these poor folks.* Then, when it seemed we were all done and it had thankfully gone unnoticed that I was B.J.'s intern and was supposedly there to assist him in moments like these, he suddenly leaned over to me and asked, "Hey Ty, you sing, right? Could you sing us a patriotic song to encourage us all, brother?" So there

I was in a crowd of mourning firemen and their families, and B.J. wanted me to somehow lift their spirits with an impromptu version of "America the Beautiful." I think I whispered back, "Beej, I'm not even sure I know all the words to that song." His response was basically to chuckle and say, "Well, let's find out."

From that point on there were lots of "let's find out" moments with the Beejmeister. Moments where B.J. would launch me out into the unknown, neither of us really knowing what the outcome would be. From ministering to the homeless on the streets of New York City to traveling all the way to Tokyo, Japan to preach to strangers through a translator about the good news of Jesus, B.J. was always pushing me out of my comfort zone to explore my calling. At first I didn't understand how he could be so confident sending me out into the unknown, not knowing how I would fare. Wasn't he concerned about the fragile (albeit oversized) ego of his poor intern? Or if not for my sake, what about how he would look if his intern crashed and burned at a task he had sent me out to do? Was he being reckless? Didn't he care? It took some time, but eventually I discovered the secret sauce that enabled B.J. to engage life in such a bold way. To B.J., God was real and God was good. Plain and simple. Jesus was not just a long-lost historical figure or some all-powerful, far off Deity. Jesus was B.J.'s friend. And thus, B.J.'s ability to trust that things would always work out for our good, even when it looked like we were "up the creek" or "out of our depth" as they say, came from a gut-level conviction that

Jesus was God, and that He was also B.J.'s friend. Like Paul said in Romans, "If God is for us, who can be against us?"

And so it was through all of my adventures and misadventures as B.J.'s intern, through all the failures, subsequent failures, and eventual successes, through B.J.'s friendship, protection, and encouragement, and ultimately by the grace of God, I too made the most incredible discovery of my life: Jesus Christ, the King of the universe, wanted to be my personal friend. I can't tell you how much that means to me, or how much it has changed my life, and I know it will continue to change my life forever. But I can tell you this: I will always be eternally grateful to B.J. and Sheila Weber for the role they played and the sacrifices they made to help me become someone who can say, "I am a friend of God."

Tyler Slade is a graduate of Dartmouth, with a Master of Divinity from Wycliffe Hall at Oxford University. After several years as an intern with the New York Fellowship, Tyler served on staff with the Fellowship of Christians in University and Schools (FOCUS), and as a clergyman and youth minister at Christ the King Spiritual Life Center for the Episcopal diocese of Albany. He and his wife, Audrey, have five young children, and Tyler is now a businessman in Albany, NY.

Brokenness, Healing, and 20,000 Men

By Paul Michalski

I first met B.J. Weber on October 31, 2003. Earlier that month on October 5, to be precise, God woke me up with either a 2 x 4 or a sledgehammer—I'm not entirely sure which because I never saw it coming and was too dazed to bother looking back. I was slammed with new realizations that 1) my marriage had been in a slow death spiral for several years and was heading for destruction; 2) my wife was desperately unhappy; and 3) I was pathetically clueless, blind, or in denial about all of it. The one smart thing I did on October 5 was realize that I was not going to be able to control or fix the situation on my own, and I decided to cry out to God to help me.

Through a series of inexplicable "coincidences," a few weeks later I found myself walking into something called the "New Canaan Society," a men's gathering in a huge home in New Canaan, CT. I did not know a soul in the room. All I knew was what I read in the eulogy that its founder, Jim Lane, had delivered at the funeral of NBC reporter David Bloom—that NCS was about men helping each other become better husbands and fathers. I was desperate. I drove up to the large private home in New Canaan, CT to see men directing traffic and parking on the grassy fringes of the road. Walking up to the front door, I was struck by the sight of hundreds of shoes left carefully arranged in pairs on the front porch. After an impressive breakfast buffet and worship music unlike anything I had heard, there was a talk on "How to Pray" by some pastor named Tim Keller. Then a rather gregarious member of the group stood up and loudly invited first-time attendees to follow him into a side room to hear what the New Canaan Society was all about.

I followed the group of 10-12 men into the side room and was introduced to B.J. Weber. B.J. stood on a chair and began to tell us about himself. The oral autobiography included a long string of identities (former and current), most of which I can't recall. The only one that really jumped out at me (other than he had been a Marxist) was one of his current roles as a marriage counselor. I lingered in the side room until the last question had been asked and the last man had left for work. Once all potential witnesses were gone, I introduced myself to this B.J. and quietly told him I could really use his marriage counselor services. After briefly explaining my situation to him, B.J. offered, without hesitation, to meet with Lisa and me on Fridays after each NCS meeting. I felt an immediate rush of relief—a professional was now going to come in and fix everything!

B.J. began meeting with us each Friday starting in November. After

NCS, I would drive him to our home; he would spend an hour or two with Lisa and me in our sunroom, and then I would drive him to the Darien train station to catch a train to Manhattan. One thing really confused me. B.J. never talked about or even mentioned a fee for his time—not hourly fees, session fees, or any other kind of fees. It was actually uncomfortable. However, we quickly discovered a mutually beneficial barter system once B.J. learned that I had a fairly extensive wine collection. Each Friday, I would tuck a nice bottle of Bordeaux into B.J.'s briefcase before he left. I am pretty sure it was mutually beneficial because I stopped feeling guilty about the lack of a fee and B.J. seemed very excited about the wine.

After several sunroom sessions as well as a few one-on-one sessions with B.J. in Manhattan, on December 5th, B.J. and I had to wait awhile for Lisa to show up. She was now attending the NCS women's meetings and the speaker was Os Guinness. While we waited, I asked B.J. how men could identify a specific date when they "became a Christian"—that was when B.J. realized that he had been making a big (and incorrect) assumption. He proceeded to lead me to accept Jesus as my Lord and Savior just before Lisa arrived.

In addition to the Friday sessions, B.J. took me under his wing and began to introduce Lisa and me into a wider circle of Christian fellowship. We spent Thanksgiving 2003 with the Webers, meeting Sheila for the first time. B.J. also invited me to New York

Fellowship dinners at his neighborhood haunt, Nicola Paone, where I met others who B.J. had helped or was mentoring. And then there were the one-on-one dinners with B.J. at Paone's where, for me, the message was clear: B.J. cared for me, and he cared for my family.

In November 2004, God miraculously restored our marriage. I have no doubt that our family would not be intact today had it not been for B.J.'s willingness to follow the Holy Spirit's call and give so generously of his time and heart to help this scared and lost young lawyer find Jesus, understand my brokenness, seek God's healing, and learn to love my wife. Although our Friday sessions ended in early 2004, B.J. continued to be a close friend and mentor. (NCS has since grown to 60 chapters with 20,000 men involved around the U.S.)

Even more importantly, the "ripples" of B.J.'s brand of one-on-one "retail" ministry spread out to our two children. In addition to our children being able to grow up with a Mom and Dad who love each other and love Jesus, with B.J.'s encouragement our son spent nine summers at Deerfoot Lodge Camp for Boys and our daughter blossomed in her faith at both the Deer Run and Tapawingo camps for girls. B.J. loved our children, too. And it was all without any expectation of treasure this side of Heaven.

Paul Michalski (Harvard College A.B., magna cum laude; Harvard Law School J.D., magna cum laude) was an attorney at Cravath, Swaine & Moore LLP for more than 22 years. As leader of the founding NCS chapter and NCS board member, he was part of the leadership team which helped the New Canaan Society transition from a regional to a national organization. He is founder of Integrous LLC.

The Bond of Brothers: Connecting with Other Men Beyond Work, Weather, and Sports

By Wes Yoder

T he good day I met Beej 15 years ago, I was experiencing a deep and disturbing emptiness. Meeting him felt like the wind of the Spirit blowing a gentle breeze on my face. I smiled and wondered what I had found, what gift had been given to us that day. Even on the first day, it felt like friendship.

This kind of grace, a deeper brother-friendship, was a fresh wind of change for me at a time of my life when I felt so empty, as so many (if not most) men do. Honest relationships are like wind driving away the dust and chaff of our brokenness. Journeys of love and brotherhood are never built around the worn-out idea of accountability or the leftover debris from transactional religion. By the time we met, both Beej and I had learned this. We presumed that the playfulness and mischief of our good Father had conspired to bring us together to find goodness that is only found in the heart of a brother, and we were right. Life, friendship, love, and all that is true have their being inside the relationship of Father, Son, and Holy Spirit, and that is where we find our brotherhood.

I was in search of a deeper freedom, freedom to find my own voice after years of helping others find their voices as a book agent and owner of a speakers agency. I needed healing after a heart-wrenching betrayal by brothers I had trusted. Beej helped me step across a threshold into sacred space—there I could associate my own humanity and brokenness with the humanity of Jesus in deep and vibrant ways, something my upbringing had only taught me in part.

I was raised in the severe yet often beautiful world of my Amish and Mennonite heritage. My professional life involved decades of work in the Christian Industrial Complex. Both are places where men seldom express their own feelings or speak of their own needs. Beej was refreshing, a man intent on being alive whatever the cost, and honest to the core. He did not hide his sorrows from me, nor did he paint an image of perfection, either past or present.

Still, I struggled to forgive my betrayers, these brothers in the faith, who were damaged and did not know what they were doing. At B.J.'s invitation and almost against my will (I hated awkward men's retreats), I found myself at a New Canaan Society men's retreat in New Paltz, N.Y. It was there that a man named John put his old weathered hands on my shoulders and said, "Son, what is going on in your life?" My tears flowed like a river as I told him. I had two men in my life I could not forgive, but I wanted to, and I wanted to be free. That was the night of my emancipation. It was, indeed, a night I found myself. That moment of confession began to stir in me a deep compassion for other men and an understanding of our mutual silence and despair, yet also that we have hope. Relationally we must travel a vast distance to reach wholeness.

I will forever be grateful to B.J. for being such a vital part of leading me into relationships with men who are not transactional (based on fair exchange), but are actually human with the Father, Son, and Holy Spirit becoming the center of our lives together. There is now a thriving community of men here in Middle Tennessee and in various places around the world who can say: "B.J. is our older brother in the remarkable journey of men being set free from their own darkness and fear."

Let the love and the peace of the Brothers continue. May we rediscover and enjoy our own child-likeness and follow the invitation to participate in the Kingdom of Heaven.

Thank you, B.J! The Blessed Peace of Christ be with you always!

There should also be a very special tribute to Sheila for putting up with B.J. and all his lousy friends for so many years! Sheila, please accept our heartfelt thanks!

Wes Yoder is the author of *Bond of Brothers: Connecting with Other Men Beyond Work, Weather, and Sports*, which was featured on the *Today Show* and other prestigious coverage. He is the founder of Ambassador Speakers Bureau and Ambassador Literary Agency, based in Nashville, TN, which led to his national media representation of many high-profile clients involved in national and international news stories and television appearances.

Calling in the Big Guns: Women

By Allison Pataki

After years of hearing about them from our mutual friends, I met B.J, Sheila, Max, and Rachel Weber for the first time in the mid-1990s, during one of their trips up from New York City to visit the home of Jamie and Carolyn Copeland. It was a cold winter day and the pond between our house and the Copelands' had frozen over, so we all bundled up and went out together for an impromptu ice-skating adventure. What I remember about that first meeting of the Weber family was just how visibly they burst with life, how genuinely they radiated warmth, and what a clear appreciation they had of joy, laughter, and fellowship.

Over the years of my childhood, the Webers became close friends, and I continued to marvel at their ability to so seamlessly cultivate that feeling of fellowship, to make others feel like instant and old friends, myself included. Consistent with that, B.J. and Sheila have this wonderful ability to make whatever "space" is theirs into a center of community and homey-ness that is open to all. One always feels welcome when in the presence of B.J. and Sheila, and that was certainly the case for me, whether it was spending time with them in excursions to the Catskill Mountains, the summer camps they introduced me to, under the bright lights of Yankee Stadium during some of the most exciting years in baseball history, and yes, of course, at their beloved home-base and New York Fellowship house on 32nd Street.

It was to this home that I returned when I moved to New York City as a young woman, having recently graduated from college and begun working in journalism in my early twenties. At that time, Margaret Copeland (also a lifelong friend of Rachel's, and the same friend with whom I'd gone ice-skating on that wintry day when I first met the Webers) mentioned to me one night over dinner that she wanted to start a women's Bible Study in New York City. I loved the idea. Though I attended Sunday service at the Church of the Immaculate Conception in downtown Manhattan, I was yearning for a more intimate faith community, one in which I could really connect with other young women and gain a deeper understanding of scripture and my own faith.

"Where should we do it?" I asked.

"I was thinking of asking Sheila," Margaret answered. I immediately knew that Margaret was correct—asking Sheila was the right way to go.

So Margaret asked Sheila if she would consider starting a Bible Study with us, and whether she would be willing to serve as its leader. Not only did Sheila agree to lead our Bible Study, but she offered to open her home on 32nd Street for the weekly meetings. That first year we put together a group of five women. The group wasn't based on us going to the same church or identifying with the same religious denomination. We all came to the home of Sheila and B.J. with different faith journeys, all of us seeking fellowship and education, prayer and community. With Sheila as our leader, we found all those things, and so much more.

With each passing year our Bible Study grew and evolved. We invited other young women whom we thought might be interested in joining. We'd gather after work, one night a week, and together we would read scripture and discuss its message. We'd pray for colleagues and career questions, for our love lives, for our families. I made new friends, and I went deeper with the friendships I already had.

I remember weeping to Sheila and the women when my mother-in-law was diagnosed with cancer and all in my family feared the worst. At that time, we were doing a semester-long study of Hebrews, and the verse that night was Hebrews 4:16: *Let us therefore come boldly to the throne of grace, that we may obtain mercy and find grace to help us in time of need.* These women wept with me and prayed boldly for my mother-in-law that night. And they kept doing that as the months passed and my husband Dave and I decided to move to Chicago to be closer to his family.

A few years later, when my husband Dave suffered a massive stroke at the age of 30 and I was pregnant with my first baby, I sat in a Fargo ICU in the middle of the night not knowing whether he would live through the next few hours. Lost in every sense of the word, I pulled out my iPhone and dashed off an email to Sheila and my Bible Study girls, begging them for prayers. At a time when I knew little else, I knew that their prayers would be immediate and powerful.

Over the years, even though our geography has changed, Sheila's presence as a spiritual friend, guide, mentor, and prayer warrior for each of us never has. I've consulted Sheila in moments of both great joy and great sorrow, knowing that she is always a willing and wise source of counsel and comfort. I've sent girlfriends to her who have needed to speak about questions of faith, and she's always "taken the call," even when those friends were complete strangers to her. I've celebrated with Sheila at countless bridal and baby showers and weddings as these women in our ever-evolving circle have marked the blessings and milestones of life.

Though I moved out of town and the group continued to meet weekly on 32nd Street, we still have this email chain that crisscrosses the country, and we pray for one another whenever prayer is needed. One young woman referred to asking this group for prayer as "calling in the big guns."

If B.J.'s passion is for people, then I think you might make the case that Sheila's passion is for purpose—both her own but also the drive to support others in fulfilling their own respective and God-given purposes. All of us who know her, we lucky people who have had the pleasure of hearing that hearty Sheila laugh, who have had the blessing of receiving that heartfelt and earnest Sheila compassion, know that it is a gift that she is here in our lives and in our world.

Allison Pataki is the New York Times bestselling author of THE TRAITOR'S WIFE, THE ACCIDENTAL EMPRESS, SISI: EMPRESS ON HER OWN, WHERE THE LIGHT FALLS, BEAUTY IN THE BROKEN PLACES, AND NELLY TAKES NEW YORK. Allison's novels have been translated into more than a dozen languages. A former news writer and producer, Allison has written for *The New York Times, ABC News, The Huffington Post, USA Today, Fox News,* and other outlets. She has appeared on *The TODAY Show, Fox & Friends, Good Day New York, Good Day Chicago,* and *MSNBC's Morning Joe.* Allison graduated Cum Laude from Yale University, and lives with her husband and two daughters in New York, where her father was governor for 12 years. Her next historical fiction novel, THE QUEEN'S FORTUNE, will be released in February 2020.

A 'Master of the Universe' Gets a Makeover

By Kenny Gestal

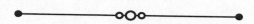

Does God have a sense of humor and a plan for all of us? So, what does a long-haired, "hog" riding, antiwar, rugby fanatic, Iowan troublemaker turned ordained priest and "street minister" have in common with a Long Island-born, Catholic school-educated, veteran, Wall Street "Master of the Universe" (in his own mind!), who is married with six children? How and why do they meet?

Let me take you back almost 20 years to a meeting in a living room in "tony" New Canaan, CT. Picture a group of men (in their stocking feet!) talking "honestly" to each other about "men" issues. Don't believe it?

Sure, I laugh and shudder at the thought of what would have happened IF I were to be "honest" with my Wall Street "friends" back then. But there was an air of trust and honesty in the room. As I listened to the stories of a couple of other "Masters"—a best-selling author and radio host, a top executive banker, a somewhat rogue priest—well, something caught my attention, or maybe touched a nerve. Was this something I might need?

Fast forward to an invitation to dinner at a local restaurant on a random Thursday night where 30 or so of these seemingly "Christian" men are talking about life and dreams. Was this weird, or *refreshing*?

I am accidentally seated next to "just" another guy (I later learned it was a set-up!), who would be speaking at the following morning's meeting. We had a very long, interesting conversation that piqued my interest about this so-called movement—the New Canaan Society.

Only later did I learn that the speaker, Tim Keller, was a famous NYC Presbyterian pastor and a nationally renowned author, which meant nothing to me at the time, since I am a born and bred Catholic.

The journey began. The friendships developed. Lifelong relationships were built.

I am pretty much a maverick type, so the "rogue priest" and I became fast friends.

Many years, conversations, dinners, meetings, and experiences later, I started to understand B.J. and his mission.

We were having dinner at La Goulue, and Beej starts telling me about this special place he goes to for spiritual renewal, and begins trying to talk me into going on a retreat with him there. I asked, "Where is there? He said, "Dubuque, Iowa, Brother!"

Sure, the "Master of the Universe" and the "Rouge Priest" going to Dubuque, Iowa, to a cloistered monastery for a week by ourselves with no internet, no phone, and in the summer with no air conditioning. To do what?

Of course, he got me to go.

Picture tiny Dubuque Regional Airport in July and I'm trying to tie up a million details because I was going to be "offline" for a week. Think panic.

We arrive at the monastery set in the "middle" of a 5,000-acre farm—a beautiful stone building built by the brothers in 1849. We are welcomed in and escorted to our individual "cells," such a far cry from my powerful and comfortable Wall Street world.
We agree to meet in an hour to discuss expectations and the rules for the week.

As B.J. is telling me, "You will wish to stay longer when the week is over," I am thinking, "What is going to be my excuse to leave early?!"

After the pep talk, we were to meet for lunch. I said I wanted to take a nap (and plan my escape!). The next thing I know, someone is knocking on my door—it was B.J. checking in on me because I had slept for 24 hours straight . . . a definite first and the beginning of a special week.

We had lunch, talked at appointment times (yes, you can talk!), and then went to the chapel for the midday prayer service. After the service, with everyone gone, I sat alone with my thoughts and decided that since I was here that I would open my mind and at least give it the old college try. I remembered that B.J.'s last words from our pep talk were: "IT ALL STARTS AT THE FOOT OF THE CROSS."

As I sat alone in the chapel, eyes closed, focusing on Jesus on the cross asking for clarity in my crazy life, something wonderful happened. Jesus came off the cross and spoke to me—LITERALLY—on June 20, 2012, saying among other things that "I AM YOUR FRIEND AND WILL BE WITH YOU THROUGH ALL THE RABBIT HOLES OF LIFE."

I was shaken to my core and changed forever. B.J. called it a visitation or "locution." I called it a life-changing conversation with the Lord. I looked down at my Bible and it was open to John 15:15: "I no longer call you servants, because a servant does not know his master's business. Instead, I have called you friends, for everything that I learned from my Father I have made known to you."

There is no doubt in my mind that Jesus is real and loves all of us unconditionally.

The brothers and nuns we met, the conversations, the wisdom and friendship that have developed are all wonderful. It is hard to explain the peacefulness and serenity of the monastery and the convent. They have become an integral part of my life, and I thank B.J. for having the courage and tenacity to bring me there.

As the week flew by and we prepared to leave, echoing in my brain were B.J.'s words from day one, and now truly, there was no way I wanted to leave. Amazing!

Each year B.J. says let's "just you and me" go back. I say yes, and each year we wind up having four to six guys in our group . . . just another part of B.J.'s ministry!

This isn't about my experience. It is about the how and who got me there. It's about relationships—with each other and with the Lord. It's about learning what God wants from us and for us and how we can learn from and help each other to those ends. It's about random and not so random acts of kindness. It's about reaching out and caring. It is about being a friend.

B.J. has become my friend, confessor, compatriot, teacher, and playmate. He has had a profound effect on my life and family. I thank him for our friendship and for including me in his sphere of influence. I thank him for the introduction to New Canaan Society men's fellowship. I thank him for our annual trip to Dubuque. But most of all I thank him for the introduction to the "real" Jesus and all the love that comes from having a relationship with Him and with each other.

I know "there are a million stories in the naked city," and this is just one of the many stories about a man with a mission, my friend, B.J. Weber. He has crammed 100 years of good works into his first 40 years of fellowship. So yes, God does have a sense of humor, and a plan for us all.

> Kenny Gestal is CEO at LQFX Technology Holdings, Inc., former owner of Decision Capital, former managing director of Swiss Bank, and former president of Sanwa-BGK Securities.

There is No Average Evening with B.J.

By Andrew J. Newell

Beej and I were going somewhere in a rush. Down his stoop, and heading west along 32nd Street, my old friend out in front of me was carving a route through the rush hour crowds with his walking stick (during his bout with a broken toe). Suddenly a BMW—shiny, black and expensive—cut in front of us as we crossed an avenue. B.J. hit the fender with his stick as it passed. I would have paused to laugh in shock if he hadn't already been ten steps ahead. We crossed 3rd Avenue, Lexington, and went down into the 33rd Street subway station. Along the way we passed a stoop where, the year before, walking quickly in the opposite direction, we had stopped in the mid-September sunset as he, noticing a disabled child in a pram, had turned back to speak briefly to her mother. "I'm a priest," he said to her, reaching out and laying his hand on her arm, before moving it to rest gently on the child. "I will pray for you both. I will keep you in my prayers." Shocked by this moment with a stranger, in a city devoid of meaningful personal encounters, the woman had thanked him quietly, and we had carried on. Now, in the bowels of the subway station he was already through the barrier, before turning to scan his MetroCard so that I could pass through as well. A permanently poor DPhil student, I can't remember ever paying for anything when I am with B.J. He won't even let me ask if I may—it's just the way he is.

He had been talking about baseball or something, and went to pick up the threads of the conversation again when, in the blur of bodies, he and I both saw a man vault the turnstile in search of a free subway ride. A hard life and bad habits made his age difficult to guess, and, although he was lithe and strong, he could have been anywhere between 27 and 35. In one step B.J. was by his side, his stick in one hand, his other reaching out to clasp the arm of this man: "Stop," he said, "you shouldn't have done that." The guy shrugged his arm away, anger and embarrassment rising in his face.

"Get off me, old man," he said in a low voice.

"No," said B.J., and then, in a moment of inspiration, "You're under arrest. This is a citizen's arrest." I stepped up behind, unsure of what would happen; everyone seemed to be watching, and somehow it was humid even though we were below ground in deep December. But in that moment B.J. had briefly lost half his years, and gripping this guy like a vice, continued to press. "I'm a priest," he said, "and what you just did is wrong man. Dead wrong." The man, who seemed quite confused, began to protest that he respected the military (B.J. wore his FDNY chaplain's jacket), that he meant no harm, that he had to get somewhere tonight. B.J. led him back through the turnstile, swiped his card to let him through, called him "son," gave him a blessing, and he was gone in the crowd.

Several hours later we were sitting in the dining room at the Metropolitan Museum of Art, arguing theology over an extraordinary meal, this boy from north-Nottinghamshire all the while wondering how many people had seen and would remember the priest handing out blessings and free subway rides, dressed in an FDNY jacket and baseball cap. The same guy who was now picking his teeth with branzino bones, and, at the top of his voice, accusing me of licking my fingers whenever the waitress walked past.

B.J.'s color and style take us places where no one else does; when it's about the spiritual life, it is rich and deep and fearless.

Andrew J. Newell is the Inkling Scholar for Literature and Theology at Wycliffe Hall, Oxford University. Andrew read for a BA in English at the University of Liverpool, and MST at the University of Oxford, where he is now a doctoral student. He first met B.J. Weber in Spring 2017 and he hasn't been quite the same since.

Destined to Meet

By Wade Kelly

Some people you are just destined to meet. If you're lucky, that guy is B.J. Weber.

It was mid-2010. I had traveled from my home in Australia and was sleeping on a floor above a church in Manhattan when I found myself getting nudged in the back by some dude in a New York Yankees baseball cap. I'd spent the night before with fellow Old Blue Rugby new boy, Antony Jerome, and Old Blue legend, Sean Horan, watching the Yankees at the Gramercy Park Tavern, getting well acquainted with American beers into the early morning on our first night in the city. Tony was still snoring on the floor across from me when this dude told us to get up and asked us who the heck we were. You can imagine after a big night out getting poked in the back while on the floor doesn't make the best start for a day. But it was a day that changed my life.

The guy with the big right boot introduced himself as the Beejmeister, father of our rugby teammate Max, Reverend at the chapel underneath us, keeper of the office we were sleeping in, and rugby man to the bone. I don't know if it was Dutch courage or I was still a bit miffed by him waking me up, but I straight out asked him: "Mate, this whole God/Jesus thing. You honestly think it's true?" He just smiled and said, "Well, if it's not true, I've just wasted my life."

I'd grown up with religion all around me, but never in me. I had a Catholic dad, went to Catholic school, Holy Communion and the rest of it, and at this stage I found myself 100% thinking it was completely bogus. I still think there's so much I don't relate to in the whole religiosity stuff. To be honest, a lot of the so-called Christian people I knew just didn't seem that great, and I thought if that's what it is, it's not for me. To me, they didn't seem that kind and were more interested in putting people through rituals that made no sense, and thought that they were so much better than everyone else.

Then there's this guy. After listening to our life stories, he takes us straight to this favorite Irish pub for brunch and orders beer for everyone. Now here's a Christian I can get on board with, I thought! Ha ha. He picked up the check and said he had to get back to work. As he left, he said "I love you guys, you're going to love this city, stay as long as you like in my office apartment, and let me know if I can help in anyway. I'll catch up with you later." We'd just met this guy and gate crashed his office. Tony and I just looked at each other, stunned. I said to him, "What the hell was that?" He just smiled and shrugged.

I had partied around the world for 12 years, masquerading as a pro rugby player when I agreed to come and play a final season for the multi-champion Old Blue Rugby Football Club in NYC. They promised me an apartment, with another recruit Tony, but when we arrived they said just stay at B.J.'s office on the floor for a couple of nights while we arrange it. We stayed for the whole rugby season.

People ask, *How did you sleep on a floor for ten months?* It's a really strange thing to explain. I have only ever felt it with a few people. When you are around them, the world just feels right. You only need a minute to sit with them and everything just melts away. In my mind, it's because they are completely content. They know the secret of life is helping others and it gives them this air of tranquility that's addictive to be around. Being around Beej just makes you feel good. Stuff like sleeping on a floor, no kitchen, no wardrobes, etc. just didn't seem to matter. Hanging out with Beej, all was good with the world.

For that season at Old Blue I witnessed this guy's amazing life. Every day, day after day after day, and every night thrown in! Just helping people with that huge big grin on his face and that spring in his step when he ambles off to help the next person. Any time he could, he helped Tony and I and every other player, of course. Even at times when I didn't know I needed help, he would nudge me in the right direction. I was no saint, but Beej didn't care. He never judged, just helped. We had some amazing times and we had a couple of real rough times and he never wavered once—just helped where he could as best he could.

Beej is just so different from a lot of "religious" people. He doesn't concern himself with all the trappings of religion—he just helps people. Every day. All day. No matter what. Finally I'd met an example of someone "being" a Christian, not just talking about it. It completely changed my point of view, and more importantly, my gut feeling about Christianity. I discovered what it was all about and in turn, discovered what life was all about. I'd heard all the catchphrases—"better to give than receive" and "the secret of living is giving"—but I'd never seen someone living it out. B.J. effortlessly does. Relentlessly.

At the end of a great season at Old Blue, saying goodbye to a club full of guys like Beej, I left New York, retired from rugby, and thought what the hell am I going to do? No qualifications, no jobs lined up, nothing. I know two things. I know rugby and I know I want to be like Beej. So, I went back to Australia and offered to coach the lowest team at my home club, just to help any way I could. We had six players. I loved it. Within 12 months I was coaching kids full-time and have done so ever since. I base my coaching on Beej. Just helping anyone I can as much as I can. I often tell them stories of the Beejmeister. It's the most rewarding job I can imagine, and after 10 years I'm still going to "work" each day and loving it. Admittedly, I haven't figured out the faith thing completely. But I have observed Beej in action, and I do want to help people like he does.

So 10 years goes by since B.J. and I have seen each other; we have had little contact. I message him: "Beej, I want to marry the woman I've been with for six years, the mother of my two girls, and you're the only guy we can possibly have do it."

His instant reply, no hesitation: "Wade, brother. I'm honored. You guys stay at my house, I'll marry you in the chapel, Sheila will sing, we'll all make dinner together, and celebrate the love. Work out the details later. Can't wait. Let me know when. Beejmeister." Nothing has changed.

My fiancée and our two young daughters came to NYC from England for B.J. to marry us. Our parents came from Australia. We spent the most amazing week with B.J. and Sheila, and as usual they treated my family as if it were theirs. By the end of the week, they are. I only find out when I'm there that B.J. is battling some serious back pain and temporary health issues. He just smiles and says repeatedly, "Love you brother, so glad you're here." That's the thing with Beej— he just gives all he's got.

Wade Kelly is the Director of Rugby at Caterham, one of the top co-educational schools in England. Wade had a stellar career as a professional rubgy player (with the Exeter Chiefs and elsewhere), and has coached professional teams. He was formerly Director of Rugby at Randwick Rugby Club, one of the most famous rugby clubs in the world.

My Lowest Ebb

By Milind Sojwal

I was at the lowest ebb in my life. I was going through severe depression and anxiety, and I was struggling with alcoholism. My moral compass was completely skewed. I had just lost my job. Waves of guilt and shame engulfed me. My self-confidence was shot. My friends had deserted me in the wake of the scandal. My phone stopped ringing, and my emails dried up. "Where is God in the midst of my crisis?" I was asking. How could I be going through this catastrophic loss after long innings of faithful service to God? Had God abandoned me?

At this most difficult stage in my life, I got an email from B.J. I vaguely remembered him. While preaching at a church in the Catskills, he and his lovely wife Sheila had taken my wife, Ajung, and me for dinner a year earlier. Since there wasn't anybody else reaching out to me, I accepted his invitation to breakfast. I arrived at B.J.'s home, shriveled by shame and guilt. I half expected some tough love and some finger wagging. Instead B.J. made me coffee and offered a bagel. And then in his basement kitchen, he reminded me that God had not abandoned me. That

His love for me had never waned and that he longed to have a deeper relationship with me. That while I was responsible for my actions, God was right there along with me—not condemning or judging, but longing for me to receive his unconditional love. I had preached the gospel of grace for 30 years. But that day I was so desperate to hear those words of grace, that I found myself warming to this man who became the very face of Jesus to me, beckoning me toward my God. Over the course of many months of weekly meetings with B.J., he shepherded me in a way that I have never been shepherded before. He repeated to me again and again the words of God from the book of Hosea: *Come, let us return to the Lord. He has torn us to pieces but he will heal us; he has injured us but he will bind up our wounds. After two days he will revive us; on the third day he will restore us that we may live in his presence.*

For my parched and dry soul, these words became like life-giving water. I drank them in and God allowed them to still my unquiet soul. I returned to a deeper reading of scripture as I found God's assurance of grace and a fuller life. In the midst of my crisis, I found hope return to me and the promise of a fuller life beckon me. I don't know if it was a new conversion experience or not. I don't know, but I know that I walked in the favor of my God once again. It felt like some scales had fallen from my eyes and I was able to see the incredible, unrelenting love of God. And B.J. had been used by God to bring hope and life to me.

Over the course of the past two and a half years, I have discovered that B.J. has played a similar role in the lives of countless men. Somehow, he seems to gravitate toward men going through crises— marital difficulties, business losses, estranged relationships with children, substance abuse issues. There is a group of young men in their twenties who meet with B.J. weekly. And he has become a father figure, mentor, example to each one of them. B.J. eschews titles like these. He prefers to refer to his work as the ministry of availability—availability to men in need. And over the years God has used him to bring men to Him who long to know more about unrelenting love.

With the healing and hope that men have found through B.J., many have gone on to serve God in incredible ways throughout this country. When you know you are beloved by God, it becomes imperative to share that love with others.

Milind Sojwal was born and raised in India and earned a Master of Theology from Princeton Theological Seminary. He served as rector of an Episcopal church in NYC for 16 years and is now pursuing a career as a Life Coach. He and his wife, Ajung, reside in Hempstead, NY, where she is the rector of St George's Church.

The Life and Death Of NBC's David Bloom (1963-2003)

By Eric Metaxas

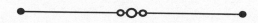

B.J. Weber and I have been very close friends for many years. We have shared innumerable ups and downs and there have been precious few friends who have been as supporting and loving and Christ-like to me during my own trials over the years as B.J. has, who has shown me Jesus in the simple day-to-day affairs of our friendship. There are few people you trust with your life and with your family's life—and B.J. is at the top of that list for me, so much so that we are essentially family. We have rejoiced together and grieved together, and I expect that to continue until we are together in God's Kingdom.

It was B.J.'s recommendation and relationships that opened the door for me to serve as the keynote speaker at the 2012 National Prayer Breakfast. So much could be said about our friendship, but one of our common endeavors, a men's fellowship called the New Canaan Society (NCS), and our mutual grief over the loss of one of our dearest friends, is a story that bears retelling.

At twelve o'clock stood New York Governor, George Pataki. At one o'clock, White House Press Secretary Ari Fleisher. At two o'clock was former New York City Mayor Rudy Guiliani. At three o'clock, just across the aisle, were Katie Couric, Matt Lauer, and Ann Curry. Everywhere one looked were pundits and anchors and government officials, so many of them that you thought you had fallen into your TV set. There was Tom Brokaw and there was Tim Russert and there was Andrea Mitchell. And there was Chris Mathews and Lester Holt and Campbell Brown. And there was Dominic Dunne and there was General Barry MacCaffrey and there was Peggy Noonan. And there we were, my wife and I, and B.J. and Sheila Weber, at our friend's funeral.

The scene was St. Patrick's Cathedral in Manhattan and the sad occasion was the funeral of David Bloom, the former NBC White House Correspondent and Weekend Today Show anchor whose good looks and brilliance and ebullience had recently brought him the greatest fame of his famous life. For several exhilarating and tense weeks the entire country had watched him and prayed for him as he bounced along in his modified tank, which someone had dubbed the Bloom Mobile, windswept and typically enthusiastic, the best-known embed in the Iraq War, updating us from the ever-changing middle of it all, and somehow reassuring us by his very presence, by his inherent and ineffable upbeatness, that everything—despite everything—was okay.

There was something inescapably iconic about David now, as if in this new role he'd become something larger than himself, as if in spite of himself—shouting over the desert wind to those of us in our living rooms—he now stood for something, something important. But what? It was as if bright and young and optimistic and brave he had come to represent the very best of us, of America—as if he had come to represent our own best image of ourselves as a people. And then one Sunday morning we got word that he had died, that our friend David had died, and for a little while, the whole world seemed to make no sense at all.

Our lives sometimes seem punctuated by these moments of bad news breaking into the delicate peace that surrounds us and that we don't notice until it is broken. I was still in bed with *The Times* and coffee when my friend B.J. had phoned me with the news. B.J. Weber was the chaplain for the New York Yankees for twenty years, but he has a much wider ministry to Wall Street executives and other professionals, and he had become a close friend of David's in his last two years. "Beej, what's up?!" I asked. He didn't mince words: "Our friend David Bloom is dead." This was the black news my wife and I and so many of our friends had been dreading in the weeks and weeks that we'd been watching and praying for David in Iraq. And as usual with this sort of news, your whole being seems to reject it instantly, viscerally, even though it's irrevocable.

Lord, no. No. I gritted my teeth and pounded my thigh—damn, damn, damn! I then got the details from B.J. and learned that David had not died from an enemy-inflicted wound, but rather, had died of a pulmonary embolism. Then I hung up and just sat there, probably for the very first time in my entire life genuinely angry at God and utterly, hopelessly baffled at His purposes. I always knew that God never fails us, that however difficult it is to see sometimes, He has a plan in the midst of the chaos; and I knew that now. But I suddenly felt as if for the first time in my life I only knew these things intellectually, as if my faith in God had now, for the very first time, been tried and shaken.

When something like this happens, it is inevitable that you scroll back, as I did that morning, to the day that David and I had first met. I remembered meeting David one happy morning about two years before, at 7 a.m. in the loud and hearty crowd at Jim Lane's house in New Canaan, Connecticut. Jim Lane was a former partner at Goldman Sachs and every Friday morning we have had our Men's Fellowship/Bible study at his house in New Canaan. It started out in 1995 as a tiny group of men, mostly Wall Street financial types, but over the years the group had grown and grown until now it was extremely large, almost comically so. At least it was comic to me; there were now about 150 men crowding into Jim's house every Friday morning, talking loudly and intensely, as though they had already been up for hours. This ragtag men's Bible study had gotten so big that we now even had an official sounding name: the New Canaan Society. Just a few years before it had been a group of eight or ten of us with me leading them through the Gospel of John. Now we were a veritable throng that swelled giddily past Jim's vast living room, spilling into his dining room and foyer; there was even a group in his library watching on closed circuit TV! And we had internationally known speakers and teachers like Chuck Colson, Jack Hayford, Reinhard Bonnke, Luis Palau, and Bruce Wilkinson. The whole affair had somehow become an undeniable phenomenon.

Every week more folks from New York and Connecticut were visiting to see what all the hoo-ha was about, and my dear friend B.J. Weber became not only a regular, but a "bringer" of friends and leaders to the group. As time went by, B.J. became an unofficial pastoral presence who was available to provide private spiritual care to men needing extra support. The group outgrew Jim's home when the attendance hit 250. They added a midtown NYC chapter, a New Jersey chapter, a national conference, regional conferences, and eventually 60 local chapters around the country, many of which have been spearheaded by B.J.'s network of friends in places like Nashville, Austin, Chicago, and beyond.

What was going on was as much like an AA meeting as anything else: men from many many miles around had heard there was a place you could come and be with other men who wouldn't judge you, but who knew we all had problems and that in order to deal with our problems we needed each other and we needed God. We'd meet almost every Friday and hear a speaker and sing a couple of songs and talk furiously with each other and then head off to work, recharged for another week. Our simple thesis was that men didn't make friendships as easily as women did, and that when things got tough at home or in your career, you needed friends to carry the load with you, to be there for you. You needed friends who would help you make the right decisions when the temptation to make the wrong one was stronger than ever. And so we had simply gotten together in that spirit, week after week after week, until things were so out of hand we literally needed a traffic cop in the front of Jim's house.

So it was on one of those mornings that I met David. I hadn't had my coffee yet and dozens of friends were hailing me and buttonholing me, and in the midst of the friendly melee I bumped into him; he looked awfully familiar, but I couldn't exactly place him, certainly not without benefit of caffeine. "David Bloom, NBC," he said, brightly and helpfully. "Right!" I said. "I thought you looked familiar!"

David told me he had been invited by a friend of his, but I didn't even know the friend's name—that's how big this group had gotten. I used to know every single person. David seemed comfortable, even to be enjoying himself, and it didn't take long for him to see that as serious as most of the men were about their faith, this was certainly not a pious bunch. Our laughter was raucous and frequent—sometimes a bit too raucous and frequent. We didn't take ourselves very seriously, but we did take God seriously. And so every week or so I'd see David there, whenever he wasn't on assignment travelling. He soon became friends with B.J. and Jim, whose investment banking offices were close to 30 Rockefeller

Center, where David worked at NBC. Through them he rather
quickly came to find what he was looking for and for the first time
in his life to finally understand the basics of the Gospel as we call
it: that faith in God and Jesus is not about trying to be a morally
perfect person. It's about recognizing that you cannot be morally
perfect, which is why you need a Savior. The simple fact is that we
need God's help to be the person He created us to be. So instead of
redoubling our efforts and failing again, we turn to Him and ask
Him to come into our lives and change us. There's a humility in
that that is the core of the Christian faith and that flies in the face
of anyone trying to appear morally superior. B.J. is especially great
at making this plain, without the usual religious trappings and
jargon, so that normal guys like David can see it in a way they've
never understood it before. And it changes lives.

David's was no exception. Through his friendships with B.J.
and Jim, he seemed to find God—and inevitably, himself— in
a way that was entirely new for him. And whenever he was at
the New Canaan Society on those mornings you could see how
genuinely happy he was to be there, how he thoroughly enjoyed
it. I remember not long before he'd left for Iraq, after a number of
weeks away (he'd been down in the D.C. area covering the sniper
case) David returned and stood up in front—which he'd never done
before—and he told us all how much the group meant to him. It
had become easy for some of us to take the group and camaraderie
for granted, so it was especially moving to see how much it had
come to mean to this man whom we all admired so.

But as with all of us who are a part of the New Canaan Society, it was and still is always the time apart from Friday mornings where the real business gets done, where the real life of our friendships with each other existed. It's in those phone calls and lunches where we would privately share our hearts with one another and where we would challenge one another and pray together and for each other.

The last time I saw David was in B.J.'s home in Manhattan. We learned that he would be leaving the very next morning for Kuwait City, and then on to Iraq. We were excited for him, and envious, in a way—but we were also quite naturally concerned for him, especially those of us who were husbands and fathers. We knew that our friend was going into the heart of an unknown warzone on the other side of the planet; so we talked about it with him and before he left we laid hands on him—the whole group of us did— and we prayed earnestly that God would protect him and bring him back safely to his family and friends.

And then, once the war started, we saw him again, sort of. I'd shout, "Hey, honey—it's David!" and my wife and I would watch him, our friend, reporting from his eponymously-named vehicle. Many of us continued to pray for him daily, to have a particular burden about his being there in the midst of so much danger, but I never imagined he would not return home. Frankly we couldn't wait for him to be back; at the New Canaan Society we'd give him a huge hero's welcome at some appropriate venue, with wine and cigars, and inevitably we'd all rib him mercilessly about what a bigshot he now was, about how lucky we were that he deigned to hang out with us, now that he was world-famous. I was already laughing about what I'd say.

Ten minutes after hearing he had died, I was thinking about that dinner—the one we'd never have now—and about the dumb jokes we'd never get to crack at his expense, and about the laughs we'd never get to have with him. And then I thought of that final prayer in B.J.'s house, and I thought of how God didn't seem to have answered it. And I for the first time in my life, I simply didn't get it.

Soon after David's death we learned that the embolism he had died from was a result of his sitting in the cramped space of that modified tank, for days and nights on end. He'd even slept in there. He had told a doctor that he had been experiencing leg cramps and the doctor had told him to take some aspirin and to seek medical attention. But of course, this meant that he would have to stop charging ahead toward Baghdad and, naturally David, being the indefatigable and irrepressible optimist that he was, elected to continue to charge ahead through the windswept sands of the desert with the U.S. Army's Third Infantry Division. I think most of us would have done precisely the same, or would have liked to think so.

I think for me it was the vibrancy of David's faith that especially made me ask why God had allowed him to die. What a difference someone makes in the world when their faith in God suddenly blossoms! You may have been some sort of Christian before, you may have believed, in your way; but then suddenly the penny drops and for some unknowable reason you turn your life over to Jesus in a completely new way and everything is new again, as though you had just been born again, which is where that overused and misunderstood term comes from. I had seen this transformation happen in my own life some years before and I had seen it happen in the lives of so many friends over the years. It's an undeniably beautiful and moving and transcendent thing to witness, as most births are. And for most people, seeing the newborn continues to be beautiful and moving and transcendent. And in a way you are forever newborn, and the world will never be the same. As Scripture says, when this happens, you are a new creature—the old things have passed away. It was clear that David had given his life over to Jesus with that great exuberance and abandon which we recognize as the unmistakable hallmarks of true love. Perhaps for the first time in his life he was truly himself, and it was a beautiful thing. Why would God have let that die?

So David's death was a particularly tough pill to swallow, and again and again and again in the days after his death, I asked God why. A few days later I would get the beginning of an answer. It was the first Friday after David's death and I was up at Jim Lane's house on the Thursday night before our regular Friday morning Fellowship breakfast. He and B.J. and I were in his kitchen and Jim handed me the hardcopy of an email. He said it was David's last email to his wife, Melanie, written twenty-four hours before he died. When he wrote the email there was no way David could have known that it would be his last email, none whatsoever; but when I read it there in Jim's kitchen that night it seemed clear as a bell that God had known. I held the paper in my hands and read it over and over and I knew that I was witness to a miracle. This was the email that I read:

It's 10 a.m. here Saturday morning, and I've just been talking to my soundman Bob Lapp about his older brother, whom he obviously loves and admires very much, who's undergoing chemotherapy treatment for Leukemia. Here Bob is out in the middle of the desert and the brother he cares the world for who had been the picture of health, devoted to his wife and kids, is dying.

Bob can't wait to be home to be with him, and I can't wait to be home to be with all of you. You can't begin to fathom, cannot begin to even glimpse the enormity of the changes I have and am continuing to undergo. God takes you to the depths of your being until you are at rock bottom and then, if you turn to him with utter and blind faith, and resolve in your heart and mind to walk only with him and toward him, picks you up by your bootstraps and leads you home. I hope and pray that all my guys get out of this in one piece. But I tell you, Mel, I am at peace. Deeply saddened by the glimpses of death and destruction I have seen, but at peace with my God, and with you. I know only that my whole way of looking at life has turned upside down here. I am, supposedly at the peak of professional success, and I could frankly care less. Yes, I'm proud of the good job we've all been doing, but in the scheme of things it matters little compared to my relationship with you, and the girls, and Jesus. There is something far beyond my level of human understanding or comprehension going on here, some forging of metal through fire.

I shifted my book of daily devotions and prayers to the inside of my flak jacket, so that it would be close to my heart, protecting me in a way, and foremost in my thoughts. When the moment comes when Jim or John or Christine or Nicole or Ava or you are talking about my last days, I am determined that they will say he was devoted to his wife and children and he gave every ounce of his being not for himself, but for those whom he cared about most—God and his family. Save this note. Look at it a month from now, a year from now, 10 years from now, 20 years from now. You cannot know now nor do I whether you will look at it with tears, heartbreak, and a sense of anguish and regret over what might have been, or whether you will say he was and is a changed man, God did work a miracle in our lives. But I swear to you on everything that I hold dear I am speaking the truth to you. And I will continue to speak the truth to you. And, not to be trite, but that will set me free. God bless you, Melanie. I love you and I know that you still love me. Please give the girls a big hug; squeeze 'em tight and let them know just how much their daddy loves and cares for them. With love and devotion, Dave.

Well. Who could possibly fail to be moved by this profound and extraordinary email? It was transcendent; it was a miracle. I could hardly fathom what I had just read. How could David have written these words one day before he died without knowing that he was going to die? It was all just too much. How could a man who doesn't know he has one day left on Earth write all of this? There was only one answer: God knew. Just as God seemed to speak prophetically through Martin Luther King Jr. in his "I Have A Dream" speech—the one in which King seems to allude to his imminent death the next day—so God seemed to me to be speaking through David here. That was the only thing I could compare this to. Suddenly I felt like I was holding a very precious document. I held the paper in my hands and just marveled at it and smiled. When I looked up I saw that B.J. and Jim were smiling, too. The next morning, instead of our usual Bible study, we had a special memorial for David, right in Jim's living room, where we had always met. As I was leading the group in prayer, I was shaking and on the verge of weeping, and as the words poured out of me I thanked God that David was with him and that that was true, that it was truer than anything we knew, that it wasn't just something that we tell ourselves to feel better, that it was not a fairytale, that it was the Gospel truth.

Over the next week I continued to marvel at that email, and I realized that it was God's way of telling us that it was okay, that He was with David and with us, that this wasn't something that had just happened. It was a measure of comfort.

Then I learned something else that was extraordinary. Jim's last voicemail to David before he died was from the April 5th entry of *My Utmost For His Highest*. And two things about the entry seemed undeniably extraordinary. First of all, the April 5th entry concerned Jesus praying in the Garden of Gethsemane, the day before his death, on what we call Maundy Thursday. And of course Jim had read this to David on the day before his own death. But there was a second way in which this entry struck me as perfectly stunning and which was most evident in its very last line. This is what Jim had read to David:

"The agony in the Garden was the agony of the Son of God in fulfilling His destiny as the Savior of the world. The veil is pulled back here to reveal all that it cost Him to make it possible for us to become sons of God. His agony was the basis for the simplicity of our salvation. The Cross of Christ was a triumph for the Son of Man. It was not only a sign that our Lord had triumphed, but that He had triumphed to save the human race. Because of what the Son of man went through, every human being can now get through into the very presence of God."

And then, for emphasis, Jim read the last sentence a second time: **"Because of what the Son of Man went through, every human being can now get through into the very presence of God."**

We learned from David's cameraman that moments after he heard this last voicemail that morning, just after he had heard that last line twice, David climbed out of the Bloom Mobile and collapsed, and himself entered into the very presence of God.

Who can fathom such things? It seems that there are very rare times in life when the hand of God is easy to see, when God almost desperately seems to want us to know that He is involved in a situation, that it isn't something that just happened, but that He was involved in orchestrating it, that He is with us in all of its details. It's at these times that you know how tenderhearted our God is, because in communicating to us that He was involved, God is telling us that as terrible as things might seem, He is with us. We are not alone. I cannot doubt that the extraordinary events surrounding David's death are a powerful example of one of those times.

Jim gave the eulogy at the memorial service at St. Patrick's Cathedral, and B.J. gave the eulogy at the funeral in Pound Ridge, NY. When I think now of that celebration dinner that we would never have, in honor of David's homecoming, I realize I was wrong in two ways: first of all, we will have that celebration, and second, the homecoming will not be David's, but ours.

"Because of what the Son of Man went through, every human being can now get through into the very presence of God."

And we will. And when we join David in God's presence, there we will rejoice with him as we never could have dreamt of rejoicing with him in this life, and our joy together will be like a waterfall of grace; and our laughter together will be brilliant and golden and everlasting. This is not a fairytale. It is the Gospel truth.

Editor's Note: Sections reprinted with permission from the *New Canaan Society David Bloom Commemorative Edition of My Utmost for His Highest.*

Eric Metaxas is the New York Times #1 bestselling author of *Martin Luther, If You Can Keep It, Bonhoeffer, Miracles, Seven Women, Seven Men,* and *Amazing Grace.* He has written more than thirty children's books, including the bestsellers *Squanto and the Miracle of Thanksgiving* and *It's Time to Sleep, My Love,* illustrated by Nancy Tillman. His books have been translated into more than twenty-five languages. He is the host of the *Eric Metaxas Radio Show,* a nationally syndicated program heard in more than 120 cities around the U.S. and aired on TBN. Metaxas speaks to thousands around the U.S. and internationally each year.

NEW YORK
FELLOWSHIP:
A PHOTO ALBUM

NY Fellowship House hosting, teaching & conversations.

Coming full circle. Father William visits men's dinners at NYF House.

Young men's weekly dinner and study.

B.J. meeting with cadets at West Point.

Two generations of young women's Bible study groups.

Bob Muzikowski (dark shirt) has renewed an entire Chicago neighborhood by founding the nation's largest little league and a private Christian school, the Chicago Hope Academy.

Father William (far left) and B.J. (in clinic doorway) formed the Amistad Mission, building a school and clinic in a Bolivian Andes Mountain village, and a model orphanage in the city of Cochabamba.

A plaque honors friends of B.J., who helped build the orphanage playground in Cochabamba, Bolivia.

B.J. Weber in the NY Yankee Clubhouse with World Series' star Darryl Strawberry and David Swanson, Sr. (front left), who was a co-founder of the Baseball and Football Chapel Programs.

"I'm here today because of men like B.J. Weber." A sober and faith-filled Darryl Strawberry shared his testimony at a 2019 NCS men's retreat. Pictured here with B.J. and David Swanson, Jr.

NY Fellowship Christmas Caroling parties.

Kern Collymore and Janene Yazzie got married at the NY Fellowship House. Now with 2 children, they bring development efforts to the Navajo Nation.

Dinners with ambassadors from the United Nations.

Sheila (pictured center) in Trinidad as B.J. coached a rugby tour—which he (unsuccessfully) tried to pass off as their 25th wedding anniversary trip!

Author Eric Metaxas (bottom, far right) joined B.J. to discuss life, God, and other small topics at an NYF dinner with the Columbia University rugby team that B.J. coached for many years.

Wade Kelly with wife Shay and their daughters traveled from London to be married by B.J. Their small wedding dinner was hosted in the Weber's home.

Small conversations matter. Shown are two Russian couples who traveled to the U.S. to learn more about ministry and church development. Visitors are constant. All roads lead to Rome...er...uh...New York City that is.

College students on tour visit the N.Y. Fellowship House for dialogue about faith and urban missions.

Friends since 1973, Father William Wilson, former Trappist monk who became an Anglican Bishop, with his wife of 30 years, Dr. Susan Winchester, still share life's profound moments with B.J. and Sheila Weber.

Weber family in 2018. (left to right) B.J. & Sheila Weber; J.J., Rachel, John, & Meira Nehme; Bo, Lauren & Max Weber. Liam Nehme and Lita Weber were born in 2019.

Epilogue

By Rachel Weber Nehme

People often ask me what it's like to have B.J. Weber as my dad. I think it's fair enough to say that being B.J. Weber's daughter is a singularly unique experience. My dad is a big dreamer with a larger-than-life personality. My parents' ministry of hospitality seemed borderless when I was a child growing up in New York City. In between friendships with our local sushi chef, sanitation workers, delivery men, and WWII veterans on our street, my father was inviting people from all walks of life into our home for gritty and honest conversation over a freshly grilled piece of meat and a favorite bottle of wine.

However, one can only imagine the woes of a teenage daughter whose father's boisterous personality comes with a limited verbal filter. To this day, before any kind of gathering where there is someone important to me (a friend, a colleague, or even someone I know who may be shy or easily embarrassed), my father and I have a very special ritual. I sit him down and make him look me squarely in the eye as I list dozens of topics that are "off-limits." Alas, this is a risky game to play, because all too often he gets a mischievous look in his eye and announces at dinner, "Well Rachel told me she didn't want me to bring up such-and-such, but I think we can all handle it, don't you?"

There were many days as a teenager riddled with stereotypical angst and criticism where I wondered how God could possibly use my father to minister to people when he couldn't even hold his tongue at my parent/teacher conferences! Yet now I clearly see his ability to cut through surface-level niceties and get straight to the heart of connecting with others who long to be seen and known. It was not always easy growing up in a ministry home. There are sacrifices that come with being relationally available in ministry: late-night calls from someone in trouble or strangers sharing family dinners on a regular basis. But I also was blessed to have a father who was relationally committed to me as well. A father who didn't let me date duds. A father who genuinely liked my friends and loved having them over for dinner and late-night chats. A father who wasn't afraid to tackle hard issues over the dinner table with his kids and their friends.

Is my father perfect? No. Is he available to God? Yes. I have been deeply shaped by witnessing what God has been able to accomplish with my father's audacious "yes" to the Holy Spirit's prompting, in spite of my father's human limitations.

I remember my dad saying, "Nobody was betting on me, Rachel." The folks in the small town of Dubuque, Iowa had written him off. He was always getting into trouble. Yet when a simple monk, unafraid of this hot-headed rebel, was bold enough to listen to him and unflinchingly share the words of Jesus, the life of this quick-tempered young man was turned upside-down. What if the monk had thought to himself, "I better let this guy go or I may offend him with my ideas?" I shudder to think where my father could have ended up if Father Mathias had decided to leave my dad alone instead of wholeheartedly pursuing him.

I now realize that much of my fathers' audacious spirit and probing questions are a result of his gratitude for the relational boldness that Father Mathias showed. That gratitude is why my dad lives with a "yes" posture to Christ, the fruit of which is so evident in these stories of personal transformation, stories which were only possible because my dad was brave enough to walk into people's messy lives with nothing but bold friendship and the promise of Jesus.

My mother also said "yes" to God's call. Little did she know what would unfold for her life on the day she married my father in 1980. In fact, she probably should have been more reticent than she was! Even though my father's sisters cornered her to issue a dire warning as to what she was about to get herself into, my mother has been devoted to the will of God for their marriage through the peaks and valleys of nearly 40 years of ministry. And make no mistake—there are two people in the Weber household in full-time ministry. My mother made the decision long ago to enter fully into a life of service shoulder-to-shoulder with my father. Her spirit of hospitality, generosity, flexibility, and relational openness to engage with diverse individuals in need of friendship are just a few characteristics she has exemplified over the years. Much of my mother's tireless and faithful service has been behind the scenes, visible only to our family, yet she has been a grace-filled and wise partner for my father.

As I reflect on the ministry of the New York Fellowship, and the countless acts of faith that have led my parents through 40 years in New York City, the main takeaway is not achieving something big for God or getting it right 100% of the time. The story of my father's call to NYC exemplifies the spiritual truth that what matters most is simply showing up, saying "yes" to God, and allowing Him to bring about real transformation. I am deeply grateful to look back at how my parents, when faced with uncertainties and unknowns, lived a life of surrender and trust. This collection of stories inspires me as I learn to live faithfully and fully in my own vocation and friendship with Jesus.

Rachel Grace Weber Nehme met her husband John Nehme at Vanderbilt University. They live in Austin, Texas with their 6-year-old daughter Meira, 4-year-old son J.J., and almost 1-year-old son Liam. Rachel has worked in Rwanda with the As We Forgive Campaign, Prison Fellowship, and True Vineyards. She is a licensed doula (birth coach), and has worked to promote Fuller Seminary's Spiritual Formation program. Her husband John is founder and president of Allies Against Slavery, and they are active members of Christ Church, Austin.

Afterword

By B.J. Weber

In 1979, I never pictured myself being in New York City for longer than six months. Now 40 years later, I ponder the passage of time and reflect upon the thousands of people I've encountered.

I had so many concerns and fears when I first arrived in NYC. During my six years as a non-vowed monk, living and working with both the men's Trappist and women's Trappistine monasteries in Dubuque, Iowa, I earned my Master of Divinity from the nearby seminary. By 1978 I was looking for my next step, and the truth is I did not want to leave the Abbey.

My feelings of fear and loneliness were resurfacing, and I recalled my earliest days in the Monastery. During one of those first years on a bitter winter morning, the bell rang at 3:30 a.m. for the Office of the Vigil, the first chapel service of the day at Our Lady of the Mississippi Abbey, where I was living in their guest house. At the sound of the bell I woke up miserable, bitter cold, and mired in loneliness. I dragged myself out of bed, bundled up in my old army jacket, and walked through the dark harsh November morning to plunk myself down on the chapel pew. *So this is what it's all about*, I mused. *No consolation, no affirmation, no joy, and feeling very alone.*

There had been recent months where nothing but darkness, guilt, and shame filled my thoughts. Mother Columba proclaimed this experience almost gleefully as "the dark night of the soul." I had read about that sorrow during my studies, but here it was in reality—dark as death and mocking me. "You fool, you have abandoned your freedom, your friends, and your lifestyle," said this dark voice inside my head. Trembling at the thoughts, I recall that tears swelled up in my heart and I wept bitterly. I wondered why. In the intonation of the ancient chant, I pleaded *O God, come to my assistance. Oh Lord, make haste to help me.* This familiar invocation is sung at every office and now became a haunting personal message. (The seven monastic offices are derived from "Seven times a day I shall praise Thee" (Psalm 118:164) and they have been traditionally observed for more than 1,500 years.)

My feelings were betraying me. *I am alone and lonely and kidding myself that I could actually have a life of love, prayer, and intimacy with God.* I began to doubt that all the sorrow that I may have caused to others could somehow be forgotten and forgiven as if "cast into the deepest part of the sea." Doubt turned to anger and anger to self-loathing. *There is nothing here for me. I have run the course and this God thing is just an illusion filled with babel. God, Jesus, the cross, the resurrection, yes, even Mary, where are you when I need a hug?* Shutting my eyes I looked up at the lone candle illuminating the darkness. I wanted to smother out that candle. I needed a job and to finish the PhD I started eight years ago, to do something—anything. *I am leaving this place. Nothing is working. I am not working. My friends and family think I am crazy.* Then I wept again. I didn't move.

From 3:30 a.m. until noon—during the next four canonical offices in the chapel—I sat and shuddered in tears. I shuffled around, went to Mass, sat down, folded my arms on the pew in front of me, and wept. Time stood still. It seemed this awful vacant dark day would never end. Just before the midday office called sext, I felt a hand on my shoulder. With a fierce tenderness, Mother Columba held me as I wept. "It's OK, Beej. The old monks called this experience 'the veil of tears.'" She went on: "Just think, you have the grace to actually share in the very sufferings of Christ. It is an inner darkness and outer pain." I felt as if an announcer was reporting a boxing match. But looking into her deep blue eyes, she radiated the compassion of our Lord. She smiled and I smiled back, perhaps for the first time in a month. The dread had passed; the veil of darkness had lifted. Mother Columba's protective love was the unseen gift of God manifested in her tenderness toward me.

As she walked back into the cloisters, she glanced back and motioned with the sign language used in the cloister's practice of silence to signal 'love you.'

The bells once again tolled. The ancient invocation and chant began for the millionth time: "Oh God come to my assistance. O Lord make haste to help me." Now feeling that I was a part of a bigger whole, I felt perhaps that I had passed some sort of test. The Lord said, "Trust Me," and it was imprinted on my heart. Mystically and wondrously at that very moment, Sister Regina sang "Amazing Grace." I was loved. I was OK. I could continue to trust. I was not alone. I knew that God loved me and provided a community for me that shared that same hope.

For the next five years, I lived in a small farmhouse near the Abbey, studied with my mentor, their priest, Father William, and worked and worshipped with the Sisters. Ultimately the silence, solitude, and prayer utterly and radically changed my perception about everything. The unseen love of God was revealed in simple things— the beauty of a flowering tree, the miracle of bugs that get ignored, birds in all their varied array, bright fresh strawberries, the beauty of wind caressing your cheek, and hearing and feeling one's own heartbeat. The truth of it was, I wanted to stay at the Abbey but knew I couldn't. There was something else ahead for me, but I just did not know what.

After seminary graduation and needing to move forward in ministry, I interviewed with a number of churches, but those jobs did not seem like the right fit for me. Mother Columba suggested I work with the poor in New York City. Upon her recommendation I called Father Bruce Ritter at Covenant House. When he learned that I wanted to share my faith and its transformative message,

Ritter suggested I reach out to the Lamb's Mission, just a few blocks from his location. Later, Covenant House became a wonderful resource and partner for me as we shared goals to rescue runaways.

So in January of 1979, I was being "sent forth" to New York City to experience working with the poor. I hated NYC. The last time I was in NYC (returning from Woodstock), I spent a night in jail. Nope, I was not eager to arrive in The Big Apple. I believed I would only be staying in NYC for six months or maybe a year and then head back home to Iowa to sort out the rest of my life. I wasn't going to be a monk, and Mother Columba gently reminded me that there were certain rules about me becoming a nun. She knew I was destined for ministry outside the cloister.

"If New York City would never be my home, why should I even go there?" I whined. Steadfastly, Columba reminded me: "To serve the poor, Beej. The poor will teach you to love, the poor will help you understand humility, the poor will teach you real charity, the poor will show you what helplessness is. We talked about this, remember? You are not alone, and the Sisters will pray for you each day."

She pressed an envelope in my hand with $500 in it and said, "We'll support your work, don't worry." With slumped shoulders, feeling every bit stupid for actually going to NYC, I walked toward my gate at the airport. Columba hugged me and gently exhorted me. Taking both of my hands she pronounced a benediction: "Remember Beej, God is greater than your sorrows and greater than your expectations."

Smiling broadly and waving goodbye, she said, "Give my regards to Broadway." The Lamb's Mission was half a block from Broadway, just east of Times Square.

Just four months later, at the end of April, by God's miraculous grace, in NYC I met the woman who would fulfill my dreams and hopes and fill my loneliness. Aside from Christ, my wife Sheila is the best thing that ever happened to me.

* * *

Never could I have imagined how the Lord has sustained Sheila and me over these 40 years, or the purposes and plans He had in store.

It has been the greatest honor and joy for me to serve Christ and to build the friendships contained in this book, as well as so many more whose stories have gone untold, but not unnoticed. I want to thank everyone who contributed to this book for their generosity in volunteering their stories.

I want to especially thank the men and women who have served so skillfully and faithfully on the board of directors of the New York

Fellowship, most especially our longest serving chairman, Robert A. Case, who brings skill sets and a professional background like few others could imagine, along with his spirit of encouragement and deep personal faith. All our New York Fellowship board members, past and present, have been trustworthy and made all these stories possible by their faithful service and generosity, which allowed me to be available to fulfill my calling from the Lord.

I want to thank my two wonderful children, Max and Rachel, who have grown into such admirable adults and exemplify their own deep faith in Christ with good-heartedness, steadfastness, and are already showing themselves as remarkable parents. With their amazing spouses, Lauren Weber and John Nehme, they are God's great reward and blessing to both Sheila and me on every level. We never could have predicted how our five grandchildren—Meira, J.J., and Liam Nehme, and Bo and Lita Weber—bring us unparalleled joy.

My biggest thanks goes to my wife Sheila, whose fortitude for hard things, gifted intellect, diligence to details, and personal devotion and deep faith, have enabled me to flourish. While I have been "out front" offering my time and availability for pastoral care, my wife offers assistance to my professional life in ways that other men's jobs don't always require. She manages our active ministry house, oversees our non-profit organization, runs her own public relations business, all while raising our children, hosting thousands of guests, shouldering the normal rigors of any family household, and investing in our five grandchildren. On August 2, 2020, we will have our 40th wedding anniversary, a day we could barely imagine back in 1980, for which we "bless the Lord, O my soul, and all that is within me, bless His Holy Name" (Psalm 103:1).

Finally, my deepest thanks goes to all of our supporters for their generosity at all levels—generosity of spirit, talent, treasure, and love. Truly without them—many of you reading—I could not have stayed the course. Your friendship has encouraged me and spurred me on. Your prayers have comforted and inspired me. There aren't enough words. I am so profoundly grateful and always will be.

Author Acknowledgments

I'm deeply thankful to each person who wrote a story for this book. B.J. and I are so appreciative of your generosity of time and friendship. I am keenly aware of and thankful for friendships all across the country which are just as deep, but whose stories were not able to make it into this book—some stories are just too confidential to share. To add other worthwhile stories, I simply ran out of time in order to get this book released during 2019, which is B.J.'s 40th anniversary year in NYC. Be assured that B.J. loves getting phone calls, emails, and updates from you far-flung, faithful friends in such places as Iowa, Illinois, Florida, Texas and beyond. If you are inspired to send us your story for public (or only private) use, please do! Maybe we will start a blog or publish a 2nd edition of this book.

I want to extend special heartfelt thanks to my excellent production consultant and line editor, Laura Cave, for her astute judgment, skills, mastery, and encouragement. I could not have done this without you. I am also so grateful to this book's super-talented graphic designer Laura Dueker, who was also a cheerleader in the process.

I share B.J.'s profound thanks to our New York Fellowship chairman Bob Case for his unparalleled capabilities and service, and to all our current and former NYF board members. I will always hold a special place in my heart for Pam and Barry Abell, the first people to believe in us, who wrote the first check and told us "go start the Fellowship!" back in the fall of 1984. If I start listing the amazing, faithful, and generous supporters of our ministry, I would surely take too long, embarrass some, or leave out others; you know who you are and we could not have done any of this without you. You were and are our true partners in every sense—support, prayer, action, service, and impact. This book is for you. I hope you are encouraged by it. Your generosity continues to make a difference to us and so many others.

Eternally grateful,
Sheila Weber

About B.J. Weber

Rev. William John (B.J.) Weber has lived and served in New York City since 1979. Upon first coming to Manhattan, B.J. started a street ministry, where for five years he served in rescue and recovery efforts with addicts, prostitutes, teenage runaways, and the homeless, while co-pastoring a mission church in Times Square. In 1984, B.J. founded the New York Fellowship, an interdenominational ministry, which provides spiritual direction, counseling, and pastoral care to leaders in the business and professional communities of the New York City area. For more than a dozen years, B.J. served as Chaplain for the World Series Champion New York Yankees. He is the co-founder of more than 25 inner-city ministries, including the East Harlem Little League, Youth Impact, Pregnancy Help, Brooklyn Little League, and Kids to Camp Program. He also was co-founder of the Amistad Mission Clinic and Orphanage in Bolivia, and has been the catalyst for launching other endeavors that reflect Christ's love for those in need.

B.J. Weber is an ordained minister, received a Master of Divinity from the University of Dubuque Theological Seminary in Dubuque, Iowa, and graduated with a B.S. in Psychology at Iowa State University. During seminary, he lived for six years as a non-vowed monk, attached to the New Melleray Trappist Monastery in Iowa, where upon a casual visit to buy their homemade bread, he first came to faith in Christ. He worked and lived for those seminary years in relationship with their sister Trappistine convent, Our Lady of the Mississippi Abbey, whose chaplain, as well as the abbess, provided spiritual direction and mentoring during B.J.'s early years in faith.

Since 1980, B.J. has been married to his wife, Sheila, a journalist and public relations consultant, who has also been vitally instrumental in the founding and managing of the New York Fellowship. They run a hospitality house in midtown Manhattan, which serves visitors from all over the world and hosts ongoing dinners and outreach events. They have a married son, a married daughter, and five grandchildren.

B.J. has received the following honors and awards.

- **The Herbert E. Manning, Jr. Distinctive Service Award,** 2010, from University of Dubuque Theological Seminary, Dubuque, Iowa.
- **Athletes and Business For Kids Award**, for exceptional leadership to rally men to action in an anti-pornography campaign.

- **Bread Winners Foundation Award**, for B.J.'s efforts to spearhead financial assistance to widows and their children who were unexpectedly and tragically left financially devasted upon the untimely loss of a husband/father.

- **Professional Sports Chaplain,** In one year alone, B.J. was the chaplain for Super Bowl XX, NCAA National Football Championships,and the National Baseball League All Star Game. He served for more than a decade as the chaplain to the New York Yankees during their most World Series-winning years. He also served as chaplain for the 2011 Rugby World Cup, the third largest international sporting event in the world.

- **Charles P. Stetson, Jr. Leadership Award,** from the King's College, NYC.

- **The Bowery Mission Leadership Award**, for helping to launch the Avenue D Men's Transitional Center, the first faith-based, government-funded homeless men's shelter in the nation.

- **Isaiah 40:31 Statue and Citation,** from West Point cadets and officers at the NCS Annual Retreat 2008.

- **Founding advisory board member** of the Dove Award, given to films for excellence in family values.

About the Editor
Sheila M. Weber

Sheila Weber is co-founder of the New York Fellowship. Sheila has more than 25 years' experience as a public relations executive and consultant, and has been a guest on more than 500 radio and TV programs as spokesperson for a variety of causes. A native of the Washington, D.C. area, Sheila has worked as a U.S. Senate press aide, a staff writer at *McCall's* magazine, an actress and media spokesperson for the *JESUS Film*, a solo vocalist, and director of public relations for a large international rehabilitation facility.

Sheila has an honors degree in Journalism and Economics from American University, and was a President's Scholar for her Master in Management degree (public policy focus) from New York University. Sheila is director of many public relations and communications endeavors—The National Preaching Initiative sponsored by The Wilberforce Forum, the Bible Literacy Project, an effort to increase study and literacy of the Bible in American public schools with production of the first academic, legally-approved Bible textbook now used in more than 650 public high schools and 45 states, called *The Bible and Its Influence*. She also interviewed and filmed historians for *THE BETTER HOUR*, a documentary film about William Wilberforce, which aired on national public television. She attained prestige media coverage for two renowned scholarly reports—"Taxpayer Costs of Divorce and Unwed Childbearing" and "For a New Thrift: Confronting the Debt Culture"—released in 2010 with national media acclaim (WSJ, NYT, and more). In 2010, Sheila launched a first-time collaborative campaign to celebrate National Marriage Week USA (Feb. 7-14) to strengthen marriage and reduce divorce rates, for which she has published many national commentaries and been featured on national TV news.

Sheila has been instrumental in supervising and managing the New York Fellowship. She serves an ongoing hospitality ministry of fellowship, outreach events, dinner gatherings, overnight guests, and hosting travelers from around the world, through the New York Fellowship hospitality house in midtown Manhattan. She and B.J. raised their son and daughter in midtown Manhattan, both of whom are now married with children. Sheila's newest and greatest joy is their five grandchildren, two in NYC and three in Austin, TX.

For more information on how to support B.J and Sheila's ongoing ministry, go to www.newyorkfellowship.org.

Made in the USA
Lexington, KY
05 November 2019